ALLSENSORS 2016

The First International Conference on Advances in Sensors, Actuators, Metering and Sensing

April 24 - 28, 2016

Venice, Italy

ALLSENSORS 2016 Editors

Paulo Estevao Cruvinel, Embrapa Instrumentation Centre - São Carlos, Brazil
Sergey Yurish, Excelera, S. L. | IFSA, Spain
Sandra Sendra Compte, University of Granada, Spain

Printed from e-media with permission by:

Curran Associates, Inc.
57 Morehouse Lane
Red Hook, NY 12571

Some format issues inherent in the e-media version may also appear in this print version.

Printed by Curran Associates, Inc. (2016)

International Academy, Research, and Industry Association (IARIA)
412 Derby Way
Wilmington, DE 19810

Phone: (408) 893-6407
Fax: (408) 527-6351

petre@iaria.org

Additional copies of this publication are available from:

Curran Associates, Inc.
57 Morehouse Lane
Red Hook, NY 12571 USA
Phone: 845-758-0400
Fax: 845-758-2633
Email: curran@proceedings.com
Web: www.proceedings.com

TABLE OF CONTENTS

ALLSENSORS 2016

Forward

The First International Conference on Advances in Sensors, Actuators, Metering and Sensing (ALLSENSORS 2016), held between April 24 and April 28, 2016 in Venice, Italy, was an inaugural event covering related topics on theory practice and applications of sensor devices, techniques, data acquisition and processing, and on wired and wireless sensors and sensor networks.

Sensors and sensor networks have a great potential of providing diverse services to a broad range of applications, not only on science and engineering, but equally importantly on issues related to critical infrastructure protection and security, healthcare, the environment, energy, food safety, and the potential impact on the quality of all areas of life.

Sensor networks and sensor-based systems support many applications today above ground. Underwater operations and applications are quite limited by comparison. Most applications refer to remotely controlled submersibles and wide-area data collection systems at a coarse granularity. Other remote sensing domains and applications are using special sensing devices and services.

Transducers and actuators complement the monitoring and control and constitute an area of interest related to sensors. They make use of specific sensor-based measurements and convey appropriate control actions.

ALLSENSORS 2016 was intended to serve as a forum for researchers from the academia and the industry, professionals, standard developers, policy makers, investors and practitioners to present their recent results, to exchange ideas, and to establish new partnerships and collaborations. The topics were on techniques and applications, best practices, awareness and experiences as well as future trends and needs (both in research and practice) related to all aspects of sensor-based applications and services.

The conference had the following tracks:

- Biosensors and bio-oriented electronics
- Sensor technologies and materials
- Sensor-related techniques and methods
- Sensor types
- Metering/Measurements

We take here the opportunity to warmly thank all the members of the ALLSENSORS 2016 technical program committee, as well as the numerous reviewers. The creation of such a high quality conference program would not have been possible without their involvement. We also kindly thank all the authors that dedicated much of their time and effort to contribute to ALLSENSORS 2016. We truly believe that, thanks to all these efforts, the final conference program consisted of top quality contributions.

Also, this event could not have been a reality without the support of many individuals, organizations and sponsors. We also gratefully thank the members of the ALLSENSORS 2016 organizing committee for their help in handling the logistics and for their work that made this professional meeting a success.

We hope ALLSENSORS 2016 was a successful international forum for the exchange of ideas and results between academia and industry and to promote further progress in the field related to sensors, actuators, metering and sensing. We also hope that Venice, Italy, provided a pleasant environment during the conference and everyone saved some time to enjoy the unique charm of the city.

ALLSENSORS Advisory Committee

Radislav A. Potyrailo, GE Global Research Center, USA
Sergey Yurish, Excelera, S. L. | IFSA, Spain
Jagannathan Sarangapani, Missouri University of Science and Technology, USA
Wei Min Huang, School of Mechanical and Aerospace Engineering - Nanyang Technological University, Singapore
Matteo Tonezzer, Institute of materials for electronics and magnetism (IMEM) - Italian National Research Council (CNR), Italy
Qingsong Xu, University of Macau, Macau, China
Paulo Estevao Cruvinel, Embrapa Instrumentation Centre - São Carlos, Brazil

ALLSENSORS 2016

Committee

ALLSENSORS Advisory Committee

Radislav A. Potyrailo, GE Global Research Center, USA
Sergey Yurish, Excelera, S. L. | IFSA, Spain
Jagannathan Sarangapani, Missouri University of Science and Technology, USA
Wei Min Huang, School of Mechanical and Aerospace Engineering - Nanyang Technological University, Singapore
Matteo Tonezzer, Institute of materials for electronics and magnetism (IMEM) - Italian National Research Council (CNR), Italy
Qingsong Xu, University of Macau, Macau, China
Paulo Estevao Cruvinel, Embrapa Instrumentation Centre - São Carlos, Brazil

ALLSENSORS 2016 Technical Program Committee

Adnane Abdelghani, Carthage University - National Institute of Applied Science and Technology, Tunisia
Khalifa Aguir, Aix-Marseille Université - IM2NP, France
Parvez Ahmad Alvi, Banasthali University, India
Amin Al-Habaibeh, Nottingham Trent University, UK
Ammar Aryan, Université de Caen Basse-Normandie, France
Mohamed Atef, Shanghai Jiao Tong University, China / Assiut University, Egypt
Yoseph Bar-Cohen, Jet Propulsion Lab (JPL) - NASA, USA
César Benavente Peces, Universidad Politécnica de Madrid, Spain
Philippe Bergonzo, CEA Saclay - Nano-INNOV, France
Fabiano Bini, University of Rome "La Sapienza", Italy
Paula M. Castro, University of A Coruña, Spain
Nan-Fu Chiu, National Taiwan Normal University, Taiwan
Niloy Choudhury, GE Global Research, Niskayuna, USA
Adriano Cola, IMM-CNR, Lecce, Italy
Alok Prasad Das, Siksha O Anusandhan University, Bhubaneswar, Odisha, India
Madhavrao Keshavrao Deore, ASC - Arts, Science and Commerce College, Ozar (Mig), India
Emiliano Descrovi, Politecnico di Torino, Italy
Francois Destelle, Dublin City University, Ireland
Lassaad El Mir, Al Imam Mohammad Ibn Saud Islamic University (IMSIU), Saudi Arabia / Faculty of Sciences in Gabes, Tunisia
Paulo Estevao Cruvinel, Embrapa Instrumentation Centre - São Carlos, Brazil
Toribio Fernández Otero, Technical University of Cartagena, Spain
Vittorio Ferrari, University of Brescia, Italy

Chemistry Institute (TPCI), Athens, Greece
Bahram Djafari Rouhani, Université de Lille Sciences et Technologies, France
José Pedro Santos Blanco, Institute of Physical and Information Technologies (ITEFI) - Superior Council of Scientific Research (CSIC), Madrid, Spain
Jagannathan Sarangapani, Missouri University of Science and Technology, USA
Irina Sergievskaya, Institute of Applied Physics of Russian Academy of Sciences (IAP), Russia
Leonello Servoli, Istituto Nazionale di Fisica Nucleare, Perugia, Italy
Arvind Shaligram, Savitribai Phule Pune University, India
Yuriy S. Shmaliy, Universidad de Guanajuato, Mexico
Marius Silaghi, Florida Institute of Technology, USA
Ingo Simonis, Open Geospatial Consortium, Germany
Norbert Stoll, Universität Rostock, Germany
Ji Su, NASA Langley Research Center, Hampton, USA
Mu-Chun Su, National Central University, Taiwan
Ramesh T. Subramaniam, University of Malaya, Malaysia
Chengliang Sun, Institute of Microelectronics, A*Star, Singapore
Ryszard Tadeusiewicz, AGH University of Science and Technology, Krakow, Poland
Pedro Renato Tavares Pinho, ISEL - Instituto Superior de Engenharia de Lisboa, Portugal
Matteo Tonezzer, Institute of materials for electronics and magnetism (IMEM) - Italian National Research Council (CNR), Italy
Federico Tramarin, National Research Council of Italy CNR-IEIIT, Italy
Magnus Willander, Linköping University, Sweden
Ling Shing Wong, INTI International University, Malaysia
Hui Wu, University of New South Wales, Sydney, Australia
Qingsong Xu, University of Macau, Macau, China
Zhengwei Yang, United States Department of Agriculture / George Mason University, USA
Sergey Yurish, Excelera, S. L. | IFSA, Spain
Bernhard Zagar, Johannes Kepler University (JKU) Linz, Austria
Lei Zhang, Chongqing University, China
Jianhua Zhou, Sun Yat-sen University, China

Copyright Information

Surface Plasmon Resonance Imaging to Study the Molecular Mechanism of Alzheimer's Disease.

Antonin Ollagnier, Eric Finot
Laboratoire Interdisciplinaire Carnot de Bourgogne, UMR 6303 CNRS
Universite de Bourgogne Franche Comté
Dijon, France
e-mail: Eric.Finot@u-bourgogne.fr

Elizabeth Drolle, Zoya Leonenko
Department of Biology, Department of Physics and Astronomy, Waterloo Institute for Nanotechnology
University of Waterloo
Waterloo, Canada
e-mail: zleonenk@uwaterloo.ca

Abstract **We have developed a state-of-the-art surface plasmon resonance imaging (SPRi) apparatus combined with microfluidics and used it to detect the binding of amyloid beta peptides to the lipid membrane, an interaction known to be involved in the molecular mechanism of amyloid toxicity in Alzheimer's disease, and to study protective effect of melatonin. Kinetics of binding was measured, and quantitative analysis was developed in order to detect melatonin partitioning into and amyloid binding to the membrane. We provided for the first time clear experimental evidence that the presence of melatonin in supported lipid membrane prevents the amyloid peptide from binding to the lipid membrane, thus gaining insight into the molecular mechanism of melatonin protection against amyloid toxicity in Alzheimer's disease.**

Keywords - SPR; microfluidics; biosensor; Alzheimer's disease; amyloid; melatonin, lipid membrane.

I. INTRODUCTION

Surface plasmon resonance imaging (SPRi) is a well-established methodology for detecting adsorption of biomolecules to surfaces. SPRi has sufficient sensitivity to detect the binding bioaffinity to chemically modified gold thin films at concentrations down to less than 1nM. Surface plasmon resonance (SPR) biosensors are widely used to assess various biomolecular interactions. This label-free technique enables real-time measurements [1][2]. Commercial SPR biosensors are capable of detecting $1 pg.mm^2$ of adsorbed analytes with sensitivities of typically 10^{-5} refractive index unit (RIU), which works well for large biomolecules. For detecting smaller molecules at low concentrations, commercial SPR instrument is not sensitive enough. We have built a home-made apparatus in which SPR is combined with microfluidics and advanced optical imaging. We developed novel statistical data analysis and achieved a dynamic range of detection from 1 mg/mL down to 10^{-15} g/mL.

Alzheimer's disease (AD) is a progressive neurodegenerative disease associated with amyloid fibril formation in the brain. Amyloid beta (Aβ) is a peptide of 36 to 43 amino acids; it is well known as a component of amyloid plaques linked to AD, with the most toxic effect being associated with Aβ(1-42) peptide and its interaction with cellular membrane [3]. The exact molecular mechanism of amyloid fibril formation and toxicity is not well understood. The Aβ(1-42) fibrillization, including the early stages of the aggregation process have been monitored using photonic sensors [4]. Melatonin is an important hormone produced in the pineal gland of the brain. It is responsible for regulating sleep/awake cycle and has been implicated in AD pathology, and has been shown to have protective effect against amyloid toxicity [5]. Although the molecular mechanism of this protection is not known, it is known that melatonin interacts with lipid membrane non-specifically [6] and may affect binding Aβ to the membrane.

We employed SPR imaging combined with microfluidics to investigate the interactions between the protein Aβ(1-42) and the 1,2-dipalmitoyl-sn-glycero-3-phosphocholine (DPPC) lipid bilayers in order to show the protective role played by the melatonin in relation to AD.

II. EXPERIMENTAL DETAILS

Figure 1 shows a schematic of the SPRi set up. The wavelength of the incident light of a halogen lamp was scanned using a monochromator, polarized, expanded and collimated using two lenses with focal lengths of 35 and 70 mm. The SPR chip consisted of SF − 10 glass slides coated on one side with a thin gold film (1nm Cr layer and 45nm Au layer) deposited by thermal evaporation The expanded beam was coupled to the SPR chip in a Kretschmann configuration, through a high-index prism (RI = 1.72) mounted on a Newport SR50CC rotation stage, allowing the angle of incidence to be precisely controlled. The reflected light was then focused and collimated using a doublet of achromatic 200 mm focal length lenses onto the monochrome digital CMOS camera (1002×1004 pixels, at 8 or 10 bits per pixel and with up to 50 frames per second).

The microfluidic cell was fabricated by molding the SU8 master with polydimethylsiloxan (PDMS) cured and baked at 100°C for 30 min. It was coupled to the chip by exerting a gentle pressure. The microfluidic cell was then functionalized with PEG-silane to passivate the inner surfaces of the microfluidic cell and all tubings, in order to reduce adsorption. The flow was generated using a peristaltic pump operating at constant flow rate of 15 μL/min.

Figure 1 shows the raw data acquired in reflection mode using the CDD camera. The reflectance R is obtained by dividing the intensities arising from the pixels inside the channel by the reference area representative of the spectral and temporal fluctuations of the light source.

Since the microfluidic cell in PDMS can swell by 1% in volume when water is flown through the channels, the reference area was taken in a bare gold area, left in the air (R = 0.9). One pixel on the camera corresponds to an area of 3μm×3μm on the SPR chip. In each channel, the data of the five central pixels were averaged to provide one value for a given length x. Fig 1C illustrates the colored image of R for three channels of 100μm width and 2mm long filled with distilled water (in blue). The surface of the bare gold film (in blue) appears to be homogeneous. This technique enables real-time measurements. Figures 1B and D show changes in wavelength with time when vesicle solution of DPPC was injected into the channel and lipid bilayer was depositing onto the gold surface.

Supported lipid membranes were formed on the surface of the SPR sensor by method of vesicle fusion as previously described [7][8]. Lipid vesicle solutions were prepared by solubilizing dry powdered lipid (Avanti Polar Lipid, Alabaster, AL) in nanopure water and subjecting the solutions to cycles of sonication and mixing. Melatonin (Sigma) solution in water was added to the supported membrane at concentration of 0.4mM. Solution of Aβ(1-42) (rPeptide, Bogart GA), pretreated to ensure monomeric form [9], was solubilized in HEPES buffer for a final concentration 500 μg/ml and was added to the supported membrane with and without melatonin.

III. RESULTS AND DICSCUSSION

Preliminary experiments have demonstrated that SPRi device is a promising sensor strategy for detecting melatonin and the binding of Aβ to the lipid membrane. Microfluidics allows for parallel experiments at the same time. Four microfluidic channels were used to detect adsorption of a DPPC bilayer, adsorption of melatonin to the bilayer, and adsorption of Aβ to the bilayer with and without melatonin. One channel with distilled and deionised water was used as a reference channel.

Figure 2A shows that the DPPC membrane absorbs the melatonin reaching a saturation point at around 3 hours. The kinetics of melatonin partitioning into the membrane was measured for the first time using this approach, Figure 2B. Melatonin saturation time is important for the next experiments when binding of amyloid to the supported membrane is measured.

Comparison of results is shown on Figures 2 A-F. Figure 2C and D show the adsorption of Aβ on the surface of lipid membrane, and Figure 2E and F show adsorption of Aβ into the lipid membrane, which was saturated with melatonin. We can clearly see that when melatonin is present in the membrane amyloid binding is significantly reduced.

IV. CONCLUSIONS

These results provided for the first time clear experimental evidence that the presence of melatonin in supported lipid membrane prevents Aβ peptide from binding to the lipid membrane, thus clarifying the molecular mechanism of melatonin preventive role in amyloid toxicity.

V. ACKNOWLEDGEMENTS

The authors acknowledge funding from Natural Science and Engineering Council of Canada (NSERC) to ZL, NSERC graduate student scholarship and Waterloo Institute for Nanotechnology (WIN) Fellowship to ED, University of Waterloo Research Partnership Grant to ZL and EF, Invited Professorship Award from University of Burgundy, Dijon to ZL, and the funding from Council of Burgundy and the Labex ACTION program (contract ANR-11-LABX-01-01) to EF. The authors acknowledge graduate students Florent Martin (UBurgundy) and Youngjik Choi (UWaterloo) for help with literature review and some experiments preparation, as well as Dr. Laurent Markey (UBurgundy) for help with microfluidic setup.

REFERENCES

[1] R. Seigneuric et al., "From nanotechnology to nanomedicine: applications to cancer research." Curr. Mol. Med., 10(7), pp. 640-652, 2010.

[2] H. Vaisocherova, V. M. Faca, A. D. Taylor, S. Hanash and S. Jiang "Comparative study of SPR and ELISA methods based on analysis of CD166/ALCAM levels in cancer and control human sera," Biosens. Bioelectron. 24(7), pp. 2143-2148, 2009.

[3] E. Drolle, F. Hane, B. Lee, Z. Leonenko, "Atomic force microscopy to study molecular mechanisms of amyloid fibril formation and toxicity in Alzheimer's disease," Drug Metabolism Rev, 46(2), pp. 207-223, 2014.

[4] S. Santi et al. "Real-time amyloid aggregation monitoring with a photonic crystal-based approach," ChemPhysChem 14, pp. 3476–3482, 2013.

[5] M.A. Pappolla et al., "Melatonin prevents death of neuroblastoma cells exposed to the Alzheimer amyloid peptide," J. Neuroscience, 17(5), pp. 1683-1690, 1997.

[6] E. Drolle et al., "Effect of melatonin and cholesterol on the structure of DOPC and DPPC membranes". Biochim & Biophys Acta, 1828, pp. 2247-2254, 2013.

[7] E. Drolle, R. M. Gaikwad, and Z. Leonenko, "Nanoscale electrostaticdomains in cholesterol-laden lipid membranes create a target for amyloid binding," Biophys. J. Lett., 103(4), L27-L29, 2012.

[8] F. Hane, E. Drolle, R. Gaikwad, E. Faught, and Z. Leonenko, "Amyloid beta aggregation on lipid membrane. Atomic force microscopy study," J. Alzheimer's Dis., 26 (3), pp. 485-494, 2011.

[9] Y. Fezoui et al.,"An improved method of preparing the amyloid beta-protein for fibrillogenesis and neurotoxicity experiments." Amyloid, 7(3), pp/ 166-178, 2000.

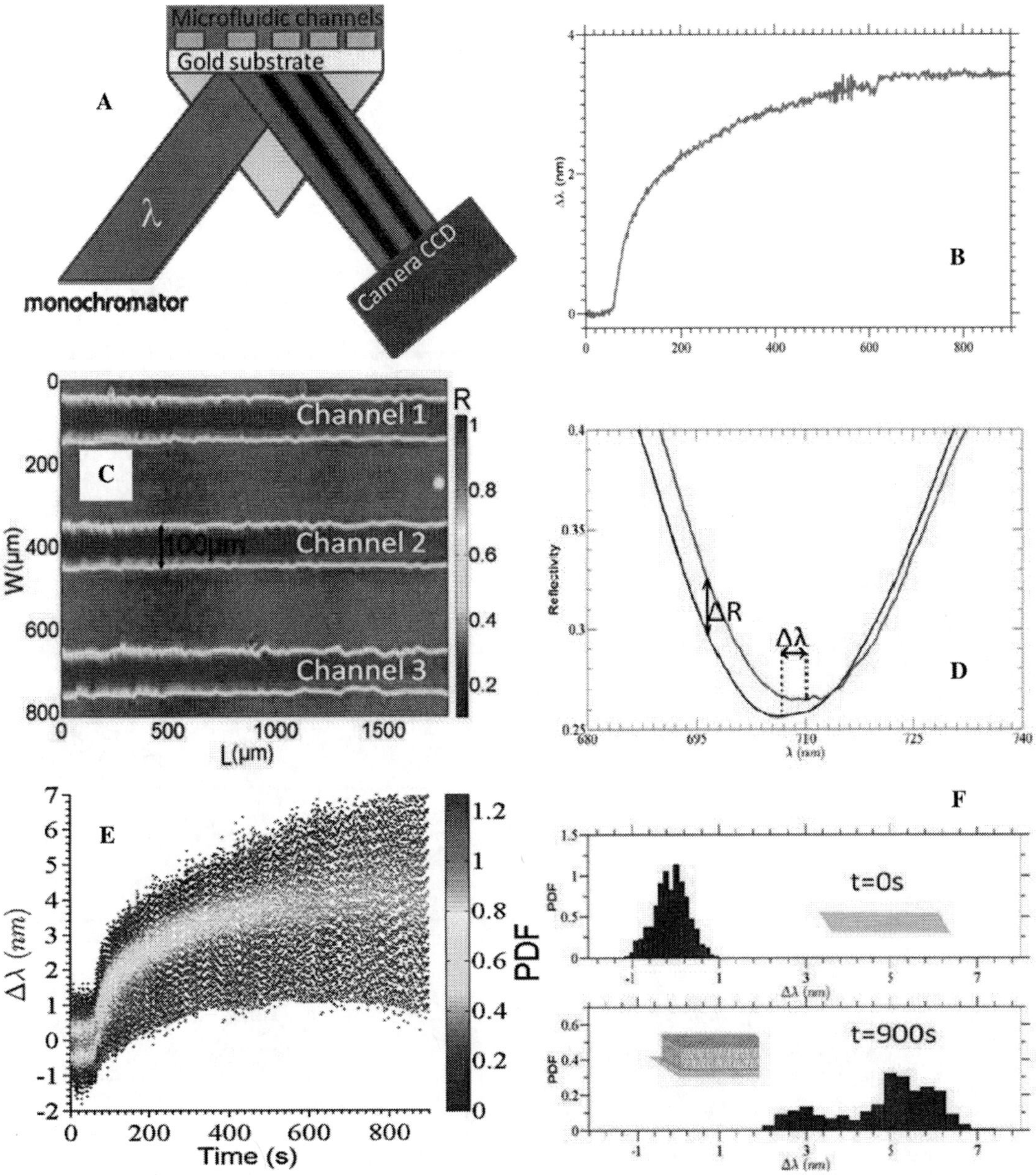

Figure 1. A- SPR set up combined with microfluidic; B- Kinetics of the adsorption of DPPC to gold substrate ; C- SPR image of three channels, blue- gold sensor surface, red- covered with polymer ; D- Spectral shift recorded before and after the adsorption ; E- Kinetics of the spectral distribution showing the probability density function (PDF) of adsorption of DPPC vesicles on gold ; E- Distribution of the shift in SPR wavelength before and after the adsorption.

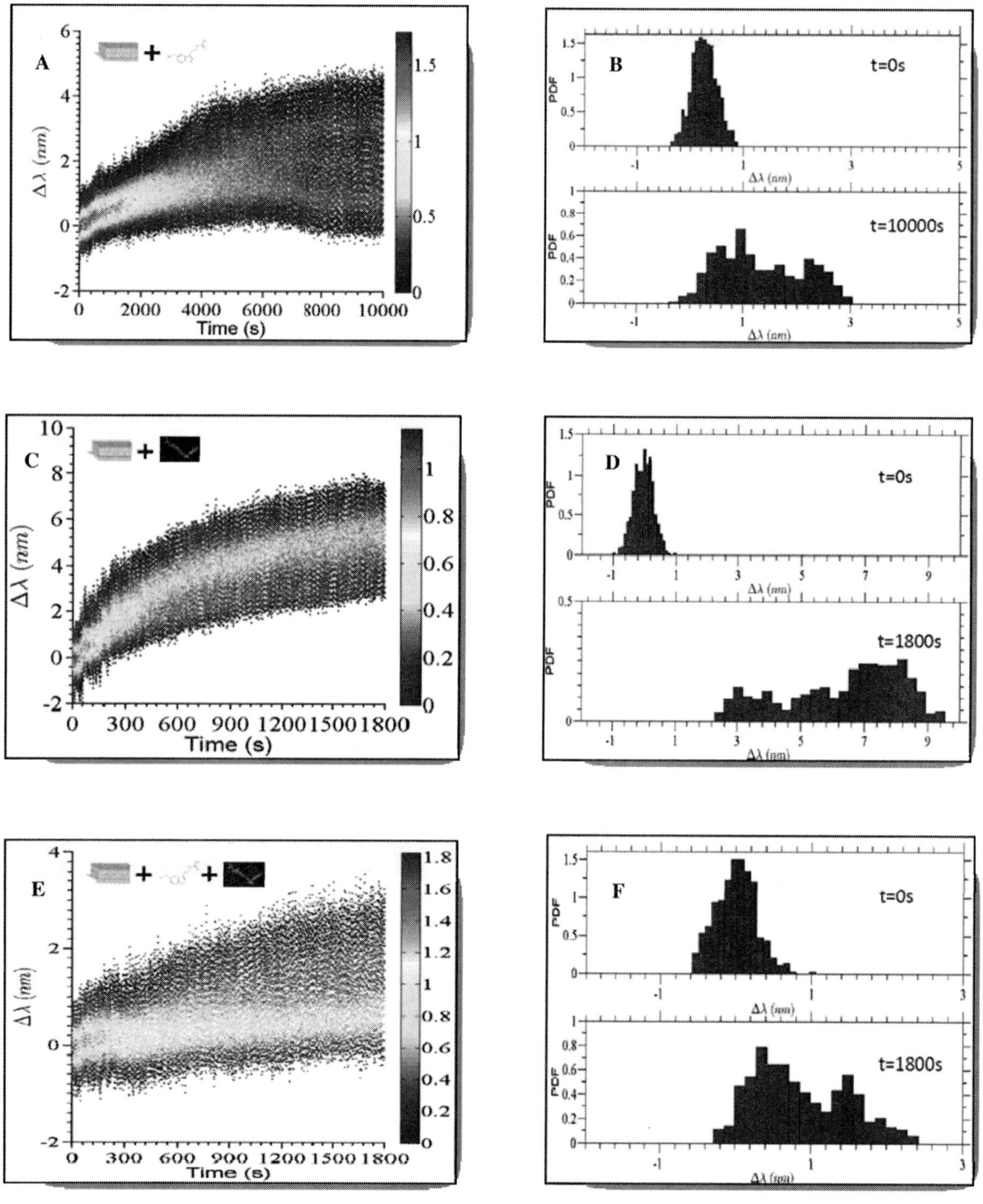

Figure 2. A and B - Kinetics of melatonin (2mM) partition into the DPPC membrane; C and D – adsorption of Aβ to the lipid membrane without melatonin; D and F – adsorption of Aβ to the lipid membrane saturated with melatonin

The Use of Bluetooth Low Energy Smart Sensor for Mobile Devices Yields an Efficient Level of Power Consumption

Khurshid Aliev, Francesco Rugiano, Eros Pasero
Department of Electronics and Telecommunications
Politecnico di Torino
Torino, Italy
e-mail:{khurshid.aliev, francesco.rugiano, eros.pasero}@polito.it

Abstract—**Mobile devices, such as smartphones and tablets have already become an integral part of our lives. For example, they are widely used throughout society with several applications in various business sectors which include smart houses, irrigation systems, healthcare and many more. This paper proposes a method to improve the use of smartphones with a smart wireless sensor network acquisition system through Bluetooth Low Energy (BLE). A new BLE Smart Sensor, which acquires environmental data was designed. This can be used with normal android devices (Smartphones, Tablets) to collect information from a smart sensor. Moreover, a BLE acquisition algorithm was successfully implemented on the firmware of the device.**

Keywords-Bluetooth Low Energy; Wireless Sensor Networks; Smartphone applications.

I. INTRODUCTION

The Internet has become an integral part of everyday life and this is expected to herald a new era of Internet expansion known as the Internet of Things (IoT). Instead of being controlled by human beings, sensors, actuators and appliances will work directly to measure and respond to a wide variety of data such as temperature, how much power is consumed, or body functions such as blood pressure or heart rate [1][2].

Wireless sensor networks (WSN) are a relatively new and fast developing area of IoT applications, which can provide processed real time data acquisition from sensors distributed in remote areas. The sensor nodes deployed on the specific places measure various environmental parameters. These measurements can help in making decisions on irrigation (automating, semi automating), fertilizer and pesticide applications, intruder detection, pest detection, yield prediction, plant disease prediction [3][4][5][6]. Hardware is currently an active research area carried out in universities around the world and in private companies. The possibilities in this field are endless due to the increasing demand to look for new sensors for different applications, the advances in miniaturization, components to be integrated, or new features to save energy. In this sense, WSN technology is clearly the most promising candidate to significantly improve automation systems of specific areas or places. In combination with low-cost communication modules and Bluetooth Low Energy (BLE) sensor motes, the new lower overall costs of WSN for smartphone applications are driving the possibility for more cost-effective applications than previously reported [7].

BLE is expected to appear in billions of devices and sensors in the next few years. The issue of power consumption of the remote devices is one of the main issues of today's IoT applications; therefore, in December 2009 it was introduced by the Bluetooth Special Interest Group to address this. The main feature of BLE is the Bluetooth specification v4.0. It is a new protocol which allows for long-term operation of Bluetooth devices that transmit low volumes of data. It enables smaller form factors, better power optimization, and the ability to operate on a small power cell for several years [8].

A different approach was used in [9], where several sensors used with different structures. In fact, increasing the number of distributed sensors maximizes the lifetime of the network, since more failures can be tolerated; this tackles the power consumption challenge. Another advantage of applying more sensors at the same time is an increased reliability of the network. The smartphone application manages the sampling frequency and the method of connection between sensors using an independent communication with each sensor, without the need for multi-hop routing to gather environmental information. The data is gathered and analyzed directly by the smartphone application. A new device was developed for data acquisition and improved android application [9] with the possibility of acquiring data from several sensors at the same time. However, hardware design and power consumption was far from optimal.

In this paper, the authors designed a completely new device which has the benefits of low cost and low power consumption using BLE technology. Moreover, we developed a new android application with the ability to communicate with BLE devices (see Fig. 1.).

The rest of this paper is organized as follows. Section II describes the hardware design and algorithm of the android application. In Section III we present the cover box of temperature and humidity acquisition system. Section IV discusses the future work and new ideas. We close the article with acknowledgements.

II. METHODS

A. *Bluetooth Low Energy Smart Sensor*

The authors of [9] presented Classic Bluetooth based temperature and humidity acquisition system. They used low power components but most of the power consumption was due to the classic Bluetooth module. The power consumption of the classic Bluetooth is 26 mW while it is waiting connection and 90mW during the transmission [9]. Concerning the power consumption of the device a new BLE based temperature and humidity device was designed.

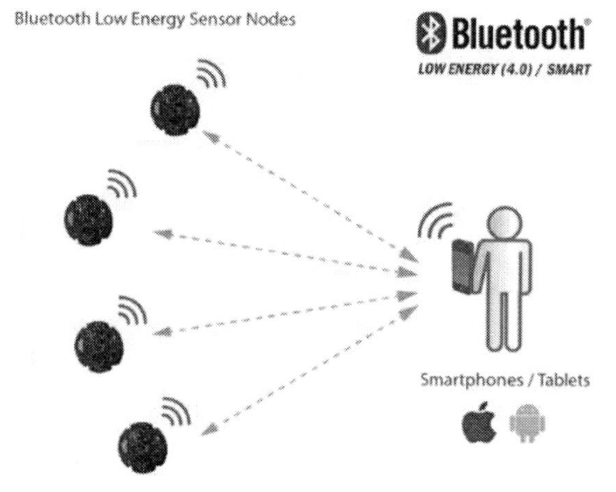

Figure 1. BLE-based wireless sensor network to collect environmental data for smartphones.

In order to reduce power consumption on the hardware part, we used a low power temperature and humidity sensor (SHT21 from Sensirion, temperature range from -40 to +125°C and accuracy of 0.3°C, humidity range from 0 to 100% and accuracy of 2%) [18]. The I2C protocol is used to communicate between sensor and microcontroller. For this system, a MSP430G2553 microcontroller from Texas Instrument MSP430 family has been selected. It is an ultra-low-power microcontroller. The architecture, combined with five low-power modes, is optimized to achieve extended battery life in portable measurement applications. The device features a powerful 16-bit RISC CPU, 16-bit registers, and constant generators that contribute to maximum code efficiency. The digitally controlled oscillator (DCO) allows wake-up from low-power modes to active mode in less than 1 µs. In addition, it has a 10-bit analog-to-digital (A/D) converter. In order to avoid power consumption, the microcontroller switches on the temperature and humidity sensor only during the acquisition of the environmental parameters; after this it switches for 15 seconds off. In addition, the microcontroller puts itself in a low power mode between two consecutive measurements in order to save power. The reasons for choosing BLE are that it consumes less power and costs less compared to the Classic Bluetooth. In addition, its simplicity, wide range of users, the capability to work in the absence of Wi-Fi and, most importantly, the fact that the new models of smartphones support BLE [10] [11] [12] are very important factors.

The BLE module HM-10 from JNHuaMao Technology Company was used to design the device. It is compatible with the new standard Bluetooth 4.0. BLE is a new short range radio technology, optimized for ultra-low power applications. It is different from Bluetooth classic (BR/EDR), but with same benefits like robustness, interoperability, royalty free or connectivity with smartphones and PCs. BLE module consumes 0.01 to 0.5 W while transmitting. The BLE module receives data from the Universal Asynchronous Receiver/Transmitter (UART) interface of the microcontroller, and forwards it to a receiver using the Generic Access Profile (GAP). GAP is the cornerstone that allows Bluetooth Low Energy devices to interoperate with each other. It provides a framework that any BLE implementation must follow to allow devices to discover each other, broadcast data, establish secure connections, and perform many other fundamental operations in a standard, universally understood manner. There is a button on the device which switches the BLE module on only during transmission of the data and turns it off after transmission. The designed hardware is powered by a 3V lithium coin battery (Energizer CR2032). Typical capacity of the battery is 240mAh (to 2.0 volts). 3D version and final prototype board of the BLE-based Temperature and Humidity acquisition system are shown in Fig. 2.

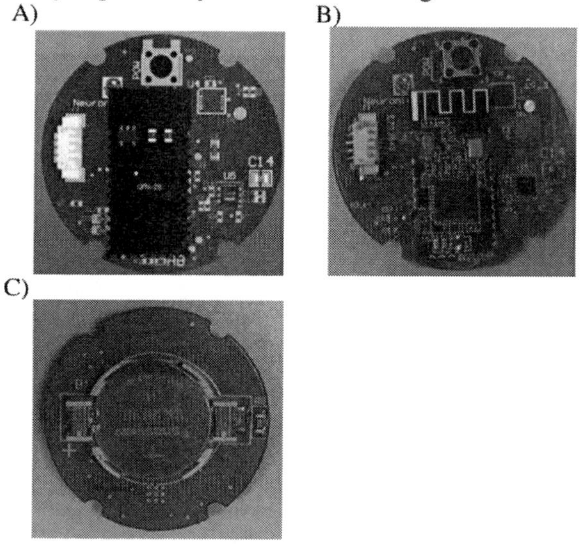

Figure 2. (A) 3D version of the electronic circuit BLE-based temperature and humidity acquisition system. (B) Prototype Board: Top view temperature and humidity sensor, microcontroller and BLE module. (C) Bottom view of the device.

B. *Android Application of Bluetooth Low Energy Smart Sensor*

An android application for the BLESensor was developed on an updated version of Android Studio.

BLE communication settings and algorithms are implemented in application. The software model of BLE is described below:

Client

A device that initiates Generic Attribute Profile (GATT) commands and requests, and accepts responses, for example a computer or smartphone.

Server

A device that receives GATT commands and requests, and returns responses, for example a temperature sensor.

Characteristic

A data value transferred between client and server, for example the current battery voltage.

Service

A collection of related characteristics, which operate together to perform a particular function. For instance, the temperature and humidity acquisition services include characteristics for a temperature measurement value, and a time interval between measurements.

Descriptor

A descriptor provides additional information about a characteristic. For instance, a temperature value characteristic may have an indication of its units (e.g., Celsius), and the maximum and minimum values which the sensor can measure. Descriptors are optional - each characteristic can have any number of descriptors.

Some service and characteristic values are used for administrative purposes - for instance, the model name and serial number can be read as standard characteristics within the Generic Access service. Services may also include other services as sub-functions; the main functions of the device are so-called primary services, and the auxiliary functions they refer to are secondary services.

Identifiers

Services, characteristics, and descriptors are collectively referred to as attributes, and identified by UUIDs. Any implementer may pick a random or pseudorandom UUID for proprietary uses, but the Bluetooth SIG have reserved a range of UUIDs (of the form xxxxxxxx-0000-1000-8000-00805F9B34FB [10]) for standard attributes. For efficiency, these identifiers are represented as 16-bit or 32-bit values in the protocol, rather than the 128 bits required for a full UUID. For example, the Device Information service has the short code 0x180A, rather than 0000180A-1000-.... The full list is kept in the Bluetooth Assigned Numbers document online.

C. *Algorithm of the BLESensor*

The Algorithm of the application: BluetoothLeService class provides a service for managing connection and data communication with a GATT server hosted on a given BLE device. DeviceControlActivity class checks whether there is Bluetooth LE communication or not and if yes display data. Moreover, this activity provides GATT services and characteristics supported by the device. The software continuously checks for the availability of the sensor and after communication it remembers the last connection [13].

The BLESensor application has a menu for discovering and selecting the desired BLE-based sensor to get characteristics. This part of the application is called Discover UUIDs, and, for all primary services, after running the application, it tries to find service with a given UUID. The software discovers all characteristics for a given service. The next step is to find a characteristic matching with a given UUID where after application reads all descriptors for particular characteristics.

Finally, GATT offers notifications and indications. The client may request a notification for a particular characteristic from the server. The server can then send the value to the client whenever it becomes available. For instance, a sensor (SHT21) server may notify its client every time it takes a measurement. This avoids the need for the client to poll the server, which would require the server's radio circuitry to be constantly operational.

An indication is similar to a notification, except that it requires a response from the client, as confirmation that it has received the message.

The next part of the application is called discovery. BLESensor can distinguish between a Bluetooth classic based device and a BLE-based device. Sensors will be saved as Pair-Sensors after each communication. After selecting sensor/s, the process of connecting starts. In some cases, two attempts are needed to connect to the sensor. If the standard method of connecting fails, the reflection method starts.

The obtained data stream needs to follow the process of tokenization to break desired values of temperature and humidity from several lines of data that are read from the sensor [10]. Acquired data is computed with the formula of the SHT21 sensor from the datasheet. Additionally, all sensor data is stored in a text file in the data storage of the mobile phone. The application has a setting to select the number of available sensors to follow and the mentioned processes will happen automatically. The main interface of the BLESensor application is shown in Fig. 3. It illustrates how two sensors send indoor and outdoor environmental data to the BLESensor mobile application.

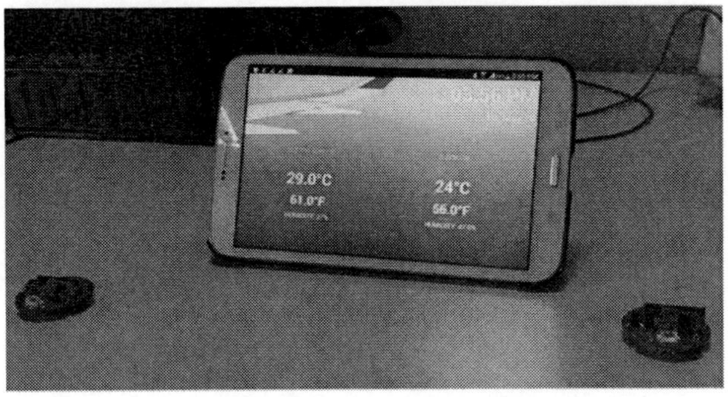

Figure 3. Main Interface of the BLE-based android application for acquiring environmental data.

III. Cover Box for Temperature and Humidity Device

One of the issues of the device was protection from environmental impacts. Moreover, esthetically it requires being attractive and easy to use for users. For that reason, we designed a cover box for the device. The cover box is designed in SOLIDWORKS 2015 x64 Edition and used STL file to print in 3D printer of Neuronica Laboratory [15]. The size of cover box is reduced as much as possible. 3D dimension of the cover box is provided in Fig. 4.

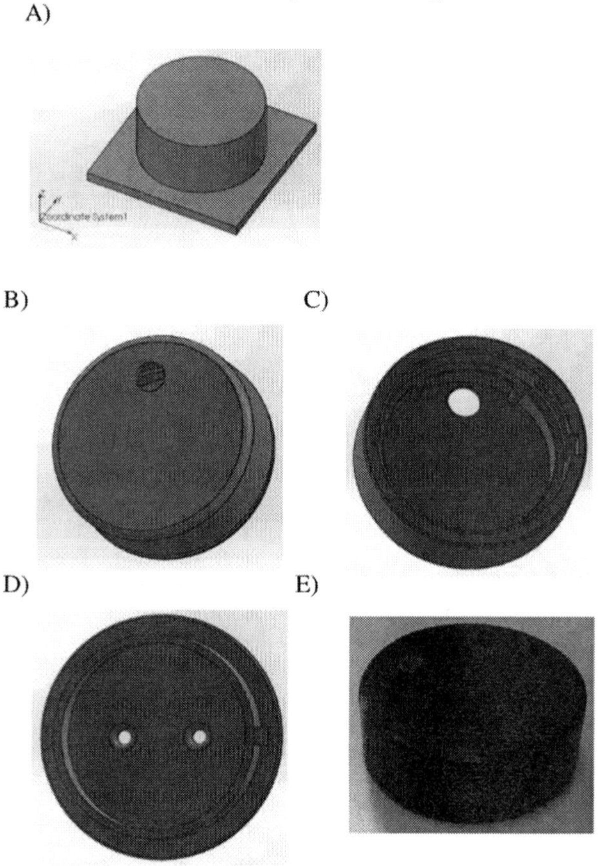

Figure 4. (A) Cover box for BLESensor: Button to switch electronic device, (B) Assembled parts of box, (C) Case of the box, (D) Cover of the case, (E) Final printed product with sensor inside.

IV. Discussion/Conclusion

This paper introduces a device designed with low power components which acquires environmental data through BLE technology and sends it to an android application developed on Android Studio [14].

Future work will focus on experiments using a climate chamber with various environmental conditions, to determine the accuracy of the sensor within it. At the same time, we will test the power consumption of the device during each condition to determine if the changes in environmental conditions alter the power consumption in any way. The amount of power which will be consumed has only been theorized at this point in time so physical data to coincide with this would confirm our original hypothesized consumption levels.

Another area of our work will focus on Network topology for BLE. This is an area of interest because billions of sensors and actuators will be deployed in the next few years and an emerging trend is to connect sensors with Internet of Things (IoT). The low-power radio technology has perhaps the highest potential for IoT use. The application which is still lacking IP capability is BLE which is expected to be incorporated in billions of consumer electronics devices around the globe (e.g., smartphones, tablets, Google glass, etc.,) [17]. Accordingly, the capability to run IPv6 over BLE opens new doors to the IoT and promotes BLE towards new application areas. The most important of these areas would be to exploit the smartphone as a gateway for providing Internet connectivity to surrounding BLE-enabled sensors. For instance, this approach allows one to remotely and ubiquitously monitor medical parameters from body sensors. Another example of the use of this application is with vehicle health messages, which can be sent by vehicular sensors through the smartphone of the driver to remote Intelligent Transportation System (ITS) control centers in order to prevent accidents. Similar applications can be found in other domains including home, urban and industrial automation. Furthermore, enabling IPv6 over BLE contributes to interoperability between IoT devices that utilize different low-power radio technologies. This is particularly important since Internet Engineering Task Force (IETF) standardization work is currently progressing towards extending the family of low-power technologies with IPv6 support [16]. Other experiments have been proposed with the goal of implementing different learning machine tools in Wireless Sensor Networks in order to predict a sensor data will also be investigated. In conclusion, the use of BLE technology with our Android system can reduce power consumption on the whole system [17].

Acknowledgment

This work has been supported by TIMUR project funded by Erasmus Mundus Action 2 program. Moreover, this project was partly funded by Italian MIUR MIE project and supported by the Politecnico of Turin NEC laboratory. Authors would like to thank Roberto Moncada and Sanwal Saleem for their assistance in the project.

References

[1] A. Zeeshan and Y. Wonyong, "A Survey on Energy Conserving Mechanisms for the Internet of Things: Wireless Networking Aspects", Sensors 2015, 15, pp. 24818-24847.

[2] A. Zanella, N. Bui, and A. Castellani, "Internet of Things for Smart Cities", IEEE Int. Things J. 2014, 1, 22–32.

[3] S. Yoo, J. Kim, T. Kim, S. Ahn, J. Sung, D. Kim, A2S "Automated Agriculture System Based on WSN", Proceedings of ISCE 2007, IEEE International Symposium on Consumer Electronics, Irving, TX, USA, 2007, pp. 20–23.

[4] S. K. Kurmi, R. Verma, and A. K. Sharma, "Modern Organic Precision E-Agriculture (MOPEA) Using Energy Efficient Wireless Sensor Network (WSN)," International Journal of Emerging Technology and Advanced Engineering.Vol 3, 2013, pp. 663-667- (ISSN 2250–2459 (Online))

[5] M. Keshtgari and A. Deljoo, "A Wireless Sensor Network Solution for Precision Agriculture Based on Zigbee Technology," Wireless Sensor Network, Vol. 4 No. 1, 2012, pp. 25-30.

[6] K. GopalaKrishna Moorthy, C. Yashuwanth, and K. Venkatesh, "A Wireless Remote Monitoring Of Agriculture Using Zigbee", International Journal of Engineering and Innovative Technology (IJEIT). Vol 2, 2013, pp. 72-74.

[7] Adam Dunkels, Programming Memory-Constrained Networked Embedded Systems. PhD thesis, 2007

[8] http://developer.android.com/index.html [retrieved: March 2, 2016]

[9] S. Aram, A. Troiano, and E. Pasero, "Environment sensing using smartphone," *Sensors Applications Symposium (SAS), 2012 IEEE*, Brescia, 2012, pp. 1-4.

[10] S. Aram, A. Troiano, F. Rugiano, and E. Pasero, "Low Power and Bluetooth-Based Wireless Sensor Network for Environmental Sensing Using Smartphones", Artificial Intelligence Applications and Innovations, IFIP Advances in Information and Communication Technology Volume 382, 2012, pp 332-340.

[11] https://en.wikipedia.org/wiki/Bluetooth_low_energy [retrieved: February 25, 2016]

[12] Bluetooth developper portal. [Online]. Available from: https://developer.bluetooth.org/Pages/default.aspx [retrieved: February 25, 2016]

[13] Safari books online. [Online]. Available from: https://www.safaribooksonline.com/library/view/getting-started-with/9781491900550/ch01.html [retrieved: February 25, 2016]

[14] Android developpers portal. [Online]. Available from: http://developer.android.com/develop/index.html

[15] Dassault Systemes SolidWorks Corporation. [Online]. Available from http://www.solidworks.com/

[16] IPv6 over Networks of Resource-Constrained Nodes (6lo). Proposed Working Group charter, 2013 http://datatracker.ietf.org/wg/6lo/charter/ [retrieved: March 1, 2016]

[17] J. Nieminen, C. Gomez, M. Isomaki, T. Savolainen, B. Patil, Z. Shelby, M. Xi, J. Oller, "Networking Solutions for Connecting Bluetooth Low Energy Enabled Machines to the Internet of Things", IEEE Network 28 (2014), pp. 83-90.

[18] Sensirioin The Sensor Company. [Online]. Available from: https://www.sensirion.com/products/digital-humidity-sensors-for-reliable-measurements/humidity-temperature-sensor-sht2x-digital-i2c-accurate/ [retrieved: March 16, 2016]

CuO Thin Film/ZnO Nanorods Heterojunction Diode Structure for Efficient Detection of NO Gas

Hwansu Yoo
Graduate School of Advanced Circuit Substrate Engineering
Chungnam National University
Daejeon, Republic of Korea
e-mail: hwansuyoo@gmail.com

Hyojin Kim, Soon-Ku Hong, and Dojin Kim
Department of Materials Science and Engineering
Chungnam National University
Daejeon, Republic of Korea
e-mail: hyojkim@cnu.ac.kr

***Abstract*—We report on the efficient detection of NO gas by an oxide semiconductor p-n heterojunction diode structure with n-type ZnO nanorods embedded in p-type CuO thin film, which was fabricated on an indium tin oxide-coated glass substrate by combining a hydrothermal synthesis method and a sputtering deposition method. The transport behavior and NO gas sensing properties of the hybrid CuO thin film/ZnO nanorods heterostructure were characterized. The oxide heterojunction structure exhibited a definite rectifying diode-like behavior at various temperatures ranging from room temperature to 250 °C. When the oxide p-n heterojunction diode structure was exposed to the acceptor gas NO in dry air, a significant decrease in the forward diode current was observed. The NO gas sensing response of the CuO thin film/ZnO nanorods heterostructure at 2 V was found to show a value as high as ~1,000% for the NO concentration of 10 ppm at a comparatively low operating temperature of 150 °C and increase linearly with increasing NO gas concentration in the range of 2-14 ppm. The experimental results indicate that this type of oxide heterostructure can be effectively used in various gas sensing applications thanks to its simple fabrication procedure and potential performance.**

Keywords-oxide heterostructure; gas sensor; p-n junction; zinc oxide, copper oxide.

I. Introduction

Recent great concern about anthropogenic environmental pollution and accidental leakages of toxic or explosive gases has led to an urgent demand for relevant gas sensors for detecting harmful gases in air. A nitric oxide or nitrogen monoxide (NO) gas sensor is much required because NO gas is closely connected with human life. Because of recent intensive studies of NO gas sensors, several types of NO gas sensors have been proposed. The most practical and effective are of the oxide semiconductor type, which utilizes oxide semiconductors including ZnO and CuO as the gas sensing element [1]. However, most oxide semiconductor-based gas sensors require operation at relatively high temperatures and have lowly sensitive responses. Recent developments in the synthesis of ZnO and CuO nanostructures with controllable size and shape have provided a good opportunity to improve gas sensing performance thanks to their large surface-to-volume ratio. In particular, a significant enhancement in the gas sensing properties of gas sensors based on ZnO nanorods has been reported [2]. Meanwhile, oxide semiconductor p–n heterojunction structures have been regarded as a key technology in many electronic and optoelectronic devices including gas sensors [3].

In this study, we report on the fabrication and characterization of an oxide semiconductor heterojunction diode structure with n-type ZnO nanorods embedded in p-type CuO thin film for sensing of NO gas. Section II provides the fabrication procedure for the CuO thin film/ZnO nanorods heterojunction structure. Section III offers a concise sketch of the experimental results for the CuO/ZnO heterojunction gas sensor element. Finally, a brief summary of this study is given in Section IV.

II. Fabrication Procedure

ZnO nanorods were grown on a glass substrate coated with an indium tin oxide (ITO) electrode via a seed-mediated hydrothermal technique with the use of a ZnO nanoparticle seed layer with a thickness of 10 nm, which was formed by thermally oxidizing a sputtered Zn metal film. Aligned ZnO nanorods were prepared by dipping the ZnO-coated substrate into an aqueous solution which consisted of 50 mM $Zn(NO_3)_2 \cdot 6H_2O$ and 50 mM $C_6H_{12}N_4$ in distilled water, and then keeping the prepared mixture under continuous magnetic stirring at 95 °C for 6 h. The substrate covered with ZnO nanorods was rinsed with deionized water and dried under a high-purity nitrogen gas flow. To fabricate an oxide p–n junction heterostructure, Cu metal film was deposited onto the array of ZnO nanorods for 20 min at RT by using a rf magnetron sputtering system with power of 50 W and then thermally oxidized in dry air at 600 °C for 1 h, yielding the oxide heterostructure with n-type ZnO nanorods embedded in p-type CuO thin film.

III. Results

The crystalline phases and morphologies of CuO thin film/ZnO nanorods heterostructures fabricated on the ITO-coated glass substrate were characterized by using X-ray diffraction (XRD) and scanning electron microscopy (SEM), respectively. A typical SEM image for the cross-sectional morphology of the oxide heterostructure is presented in Figure 1. It is clearly seen that the surface of the distinct ITO layer is covered by vertically aligned ZnO nanorods with a length of approximately 500 nm and an average diameter of approximately 40 nm. Also, an apparently blurred interface between ZnO nanorods and CuO thin film is observed with a thickness of approximately 300 nm, revealing the formation of a structure in which the ZnO nanorods are embedded in the CuO thin film. XRD was used to verify the formation of CuO and ZnO crystalline phases, showing the diffraction peaks which simply correspond to either monoclinic tenorite CuO or hexagonal wurtzite ZnO phase without any other second phase peaks being detected, as shown in Figure 2.

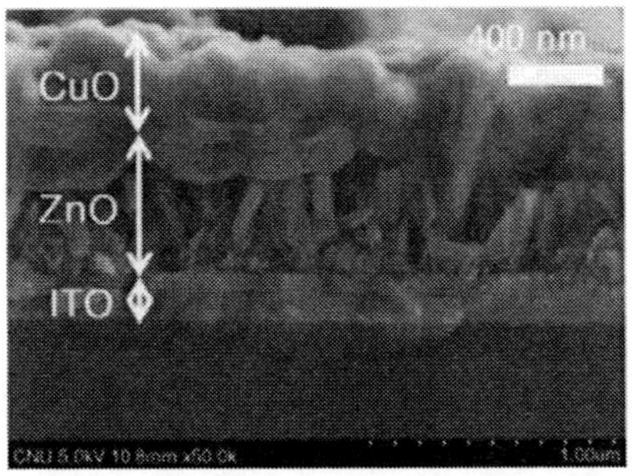

Figure 1. Cross-sectional SEM image of the CuO thin film/ZnO nanorods heterostructure fabricated on an ITO-coated glass substrate.

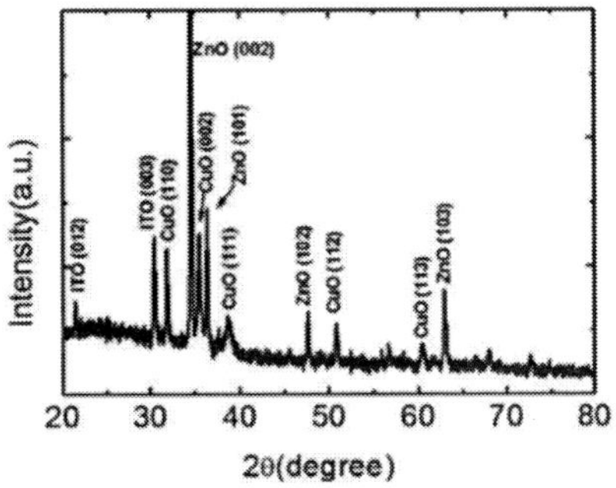

Figure 2. Typical X-ray diffraction pattern of the CuO thin film/ZnO nanorods heterostructure fabricated on an ITO-coated glass substrate.

The formation of p–n heterojunction diode structure can be confirmed by the *I–V* characteristic curves as presented in Figure 3, the inset of which shows a schematic circuit of the oxide heterostructure. Here, for electrical measurements, two square silver contacts with an area of 1×1 cm^2 were formed on CuO and ITO surfaces. All of the *I–V* characteristic curves observed in dry air at several temperatures exhibit a well-defined rectifying diode-like behavior, revealing a typical semiconductor p–n junction. With increasing the temperature, the turn-on voltage of the p-n heterojunction diode gradually decreases while its forward current distinctly increases, as expected for semiconducting materials.

In order to see the potential for gas sensing, the CuO thin film/ZnO nanorods heterostructure was exposed to NO gas in dry air. During the electrical measurements, the NO gas concentration in dry air was varied from 2 ppm to 14 ppm. Figure 4(a) illustrates the effect of NO gas concentration in dry air on the *I–V* characteristics of the oxide heterostructure at an operating temperature of 150 °C. It is clearly seen that the oxide p–n junction heterostructure exhibits a diode-like nature in the examined NO concentration range. The forward current of the oxide heterojunction diode is found to decrease significantly with the increase in NO gas concentration. Now the gas sensing response S of a p–n heterojunction structure can be estimated using the formula $S = \Delta I/I_g = (I_a - I_g)/I_g$ where I_a and I_g are the forward currents at a specific forward voltage (e.g., 2 V) in dry air and upon exposure to NO gas in dry air, respectively.

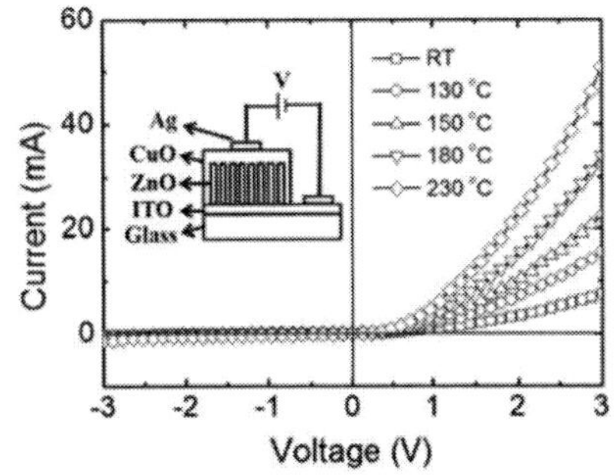

Figure 3. Current–voltage (*I–V*) characteristic curves of the CuO thin film/ZnO nanorods heterostructure in dry air at several temperatures. The inset shows a schematic circuit of the oxide p-n heterojunction device.

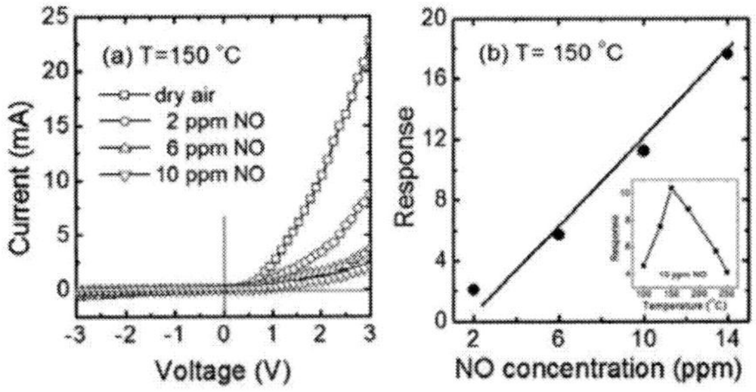

Figure 4. (a) Current–voltage (*I–V*) characteristic curves of the CuO thin film/ZnO nanorods heterojunction diode structure for several NO gas concentration in dry air at 150 °C. (b) Variation of the sensitivity as a function of the NO gas concentration in dry air.

Figure 4(b) illustrates the variation of the NO gas sensing response of the oxide heterojunction diode operating at 150 °C as a function of the NO concentration in dry air for a forward bias of 2 V, revealing a good linear relationship between gas sensing response and NO concentration. Now the observed value of the response of the CuO/ZnO hetero-junction NO gas sensor was estimated to be as high as ~1,000% for 10 ppm NO concentration at 150 °C, which is several times higher than the values observed for conventional CuO film NO gas sensors. The NO gas sensing response of the oxide heterojunction was also found to depend on the operating temperature and reach a maximum value at 150 °C, as shown in the inset of Figure 4(b).

IV. CONCLUSION

In summary, we fabricated an oxide p–n heterojunction diode structure with n-type ZnO nanorods embedded in p-type CuO thin film for efficient sensing of NO gas. The CuO thin film/ZnO nanorods heterojunction structure showed a good rectifying behavior and a significant decrease in the forward diode current upon exposure to NO gas in dry air. The NO gas sensing response of the oxide diode structure at 2 V was found to show a value as high as ~1,000% for 10 ppm NO concentration at 150 °C. This work suggests that this type of oxide heterojunction diode structure could be effectively used in various gas-sensing applications thanks to its simple fabrication procedure and good performance.

ACKNOWLEDGMENT

This study was supported by the National Research Lab Program and by a grant funded by the National Research Foundation of Korea (NRF-2013R1A1A4A01007571).

REFERENCES

[1] N. Yamazoe, G. Sakai, and K. Simanoe, "Oxide semiconductor gas sensors," Catalysis Surveys from Asia, vol. 7, April 2003, pp. 63–75.

[2] J. X. Wang *et al.*, "Hydrothermally grown oriented ZnO nanorod arrays for gas sensing applications," Nanotechnology, vol 17, September 2006, pp. 4995-4998.

[3] S. Mridha and D. Basak, "Investigation of a p-CuO/n-ZnO thin film heterojunction for H_2 gas-sensor applications," Semicond. Sci. Technol., vol. 21, June 2006, pp. 928-932.

Micro-lens as a Sensor for Detecting Variations of Solution Concentration in Inhomogeneous Medium with Time/Region/Temperature

Jiang He[a], Chan-Yuan Tan[b], Liang-Yue Yue[c], Yao-Xiong Huang[d]*
Department of Biomedical Engineering
Ji Nan University
Guang Zhou, China
e-mail: [a]hejiang106@126.com; [b]277144789@126.com; [c]yxhuang@126.com; [d]tyxhuang@jnu.edu.cn

***Abstract*—We report here a novel optical sensor technology which uses micro-lens as the sensor to perform real time monitoring of the Refractive Index (RI) of a solution, and the applications of the method in detecting the local concentration variation with time and temperature in inhomogeneous solutions.**

Keywords-Micro-lens; refractive index; temperature; solution concentration

I. INTRODUCTION

The concentration variations of solutions with temperature are important topics in biomedical research [1][2]. Since optical methods have the advantage of performing fast and accurate measurements without perturbation, they have been a powerful tool in measuring the refractive index of solutions [3][4]. Based on our previous RI detection method using microspheres [5], the present paper developed a new type of RI measurement technology which uses micro-lens for imaging and has higher precision to measure the local concentration variation in inhomogeneous solutions.

II. EXPERIMENT

A. Principle

As microsphere is RI sensor in inhomogeneous media [5], when a micro-lens is immersed in a liquid medium and illuminated by a parallel light propagating along its optical axis, a dark ring appears in the image of the micro-lens if there is a difference between the refractive index of the micro-lens n_2 and the refractive index of the surrounding medium n_1, as shown in Figure 1. Therefore, by using a micro-lens with known refractive index n_2 and measuring the ratio X (r/R) from the image of the micro-lens, one can easily determine the refractive index n_1 of its surrounding medium with the following equation (length of the micro-lens is 2.5 folds of radius):

$$n_1 = n_2 \times (13.172968X^8 + 67.604493X^7 - 150.372939X^6 + 189.176433X^5 - 147.260928X^4 + 72.6673X^3 - 22.408722X^2 + 4.408178X + 0.359321) \quad (1)$$

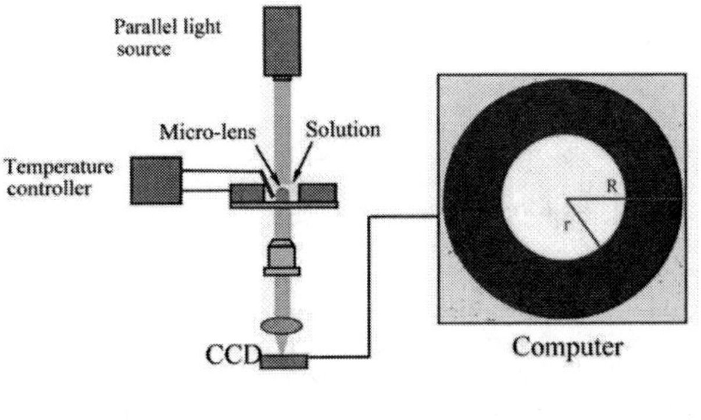

Figure 1. Schematic diagram of the measuring system and the image of a micro-lens immersed in solution.

B. Setup of the measurement

The measuring setup is shown in Figure 1. The parallel light from a LED light source is incident to the microsphere which was immersed in the target micro-region of an inhomogeneous solution, and the image of the micro-lens was taken by a CCD camera via a 40× objective. The r and R values of the micro-lens' image were measured using a homemade image processing software with a calibrated scale.

III. RESULTS AND DISCUSSION

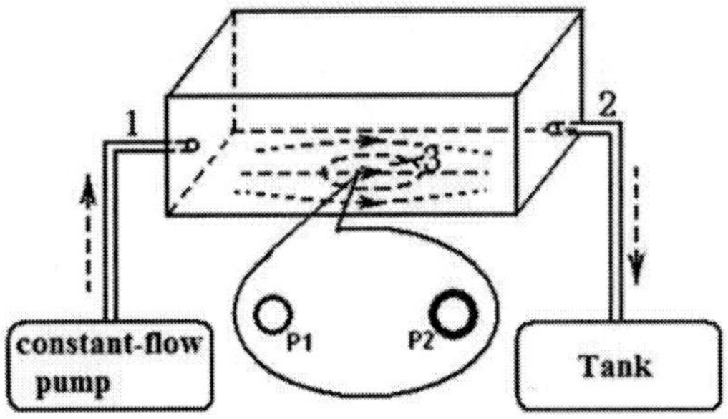

Figure 2. Two micro-lenses were used to monitor the variations of normal saline in a cell-culturing pool.

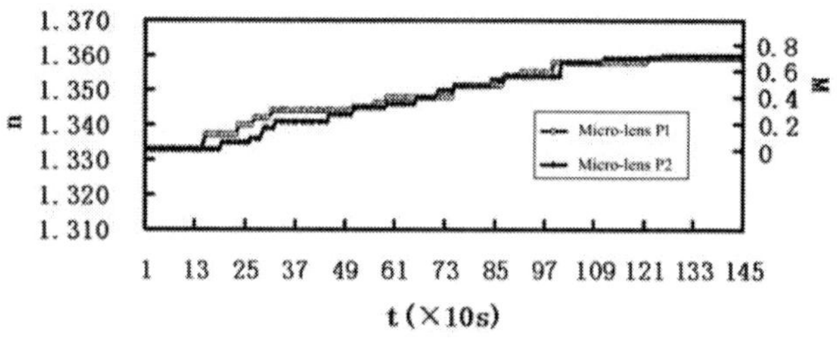

Figure 3. The variations of the refractive indices and the mole fraction (M) of the normal saline at the two micro-regions monitored by P1 and P2 respectively.

Figure 2 shows a setup of using micro-lenses to monitor the variations of local solution concentrations in micro-regions within a cell-culturing pool. The micro-lenses P1 and P2 were 50 μm in diameterandthey were separated by a distance of 200 μm. A constant-flow pump perfused normal saline into the pool. Figure 3 illustrates the variations of the refractive indices and the mole fraction (M) of the normal saline with time at the two micro-regions monitored by P1 and P2, respectively; it gives detailed information about the dynamic process of the diffusion. We can see that though the two micro-regions were just separated by a small distance of 200 μm, their normal saline concentrations were slightly different and had different rates of incensement. Since the micro-lens sensor was demonstrated to be able to detect refractive index change to as small as 10^{-5} or even to 10^{-6}, it has high resolution power to distinguish small changes in concentration. Its small size also enables it to identify the slight differences of concentration in the micro-regions separated by distance as small as ~100 μm.

By placing a silica microsphere beside the micro-lenses P1 and P2 as the sensor of the local temperature, we could determine the real-time local temperature variation. By this means, we obtained the refractive index variations of NaCl as a function of both concentration and temperature, as shown in Figure 4.

IV. CONCLUSION

In summary, we have developed a micro-lens imaging method for measuring the liquid RI. It can measure trace liquid RI accurately, and monitor the instantaneous concentration variation in different micro regions. Since the refractive index of a solution is a function of the solute concentration and temperature [6], by using our method, micro-lens can be considered as sensitive and accurate sensors for monitoring concentration and temperature variations in different regions within an inhomogeneous solution.

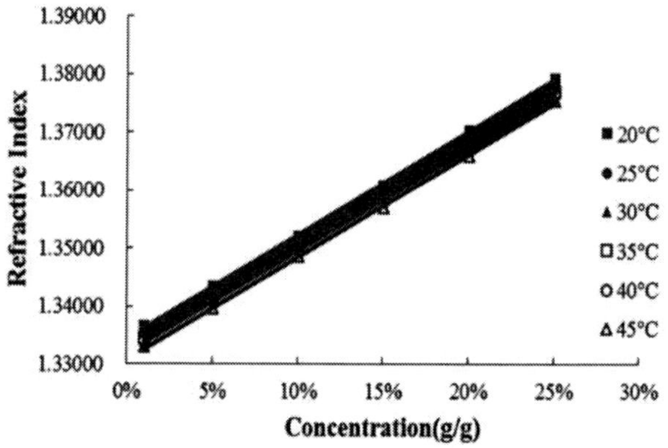

Figure 4. Refractive index of NaCl in solution as a function of concentration and temperature. RI of different concentration solution were determined at different temperature by micro-lens.

REFERENCES

[1] B.H. Weigl and P. Yager, "Microfluidic diffusion-based separation and detection," Science, Vol. 283, 1999, pp: 346-347.

[2] D. Roy, J.N. Cambre and B.S. Sumerlin, "Triply-responsive boronic acid block copolymers: solution self-assembly induced by changes in temperature, pH, or sugar concentration," Chemical Communications, Vol. 16,2009, pp: 2106-2108.

[3] H. Meng, W. Shen, G. Zhang, X. Wu, W. Wang, C. Tan, et al., "Michelson interferometer-based fiber-optic sensing of liquid refractive index," Sensors and Actuators B: Chemical, Vol. 160, 2011, pp: 720-723.

[4] J. He, W. Liu and Y.-X. Huang, "Simultaneous determination of glass transition temperatures of several polymers," PloS one, Vol. 11, 2016, pp: 1-12.

[5] L.-Y. Yue, P. Wang and Y.-X. Huang, "Easy method to determine refractive indices of microspheres and in micro-regions of inhomogeneous media," Biosensors and Bioelectronics, Vol. 30, 2011, pp: 216-222.

[5] C.-Y. Tan and Y.-X. Huang, "Dependence of refractive index on concentration and temperature in electrolyte solution, polar solution, nonpolar solution, and protein solution," Journal of Chemical & Engineering Data, Vol. 60, 2015, pp: 2827-2833.

On Line E-Nose Technology for Safety and Quality Evaluation in Cereal Processing

Federica Cheli, Luciano Pinotti, Matteo Ottoboni, Marco Tretola, Vittorio Dell'Orto
Department of Health, Animal Science and Food Safety Milano, Italy
Email: federica.cheli@unimi.it, luciano.pinotti@unimi.it, matteo.ottoboni@unimi.it, marco.tretola@unimi.it, vittorio.dellorto@unimi.it

Abstract - **The objective of this idea is to set up an electronic nose (e-nose) for the safety and quality evaluation of cereal products and by-products, focusing on mycotoxin contamination. The final goal is to evaluate the potential application of the e-nose technology as an on-line continuous monitoring and controlling tool in cereal processing, in particular wheat milling. E-nose could be integrated with other on-line analysis devices in a technological platform for monitoring and controlling food quality. Multi-sensor-devices and multi-sensor-data-fusion technology have a great potential value to the food industry to ensure that cereal products and by-products meet specifications according to their specific use.**

Keywords-Food safety; Mycotoxins; Electronic nose;

I. INTRODUCTION

During the last twenty years, the term food quality has assumed a new and more complex meaning. Topics such as sensory characteristics of a product (odour, colour and outer appearance), food safety, traceability or best practice are of great importance to today's food industry. Many different sensing methodologies represent fast and precise potential tools for "total quality" evaluation, assurance and compliance with labelling. The applications of the electronic nose (e-nose) are numerous in several areas related to the food industry, mainly in the field of quality and authenticity evaluation of fish, meat, milk, wine, coffee and tea.

Among the most important risks associated to cereals' consumption are mycotoxins. Mycotoxins are metabolites of fungi capable of having acute and chronic toxic effects. Globally, mycotoxins have a significant impact on human and animal health, economies and international trade [1]. Cereals and cereal by-products constitute a major part of the daily diet of humans and animals. Food processing affects mycotoxin distribution and concentration. Cereal processes reduce and concentrate mycotoxins into fractions that are commonly used for humans and as animal feed, respectively. A wide range of analytical methods for mycotoxin determination in food has been developed in recent years [2]. At the industry level, the adoption of a rapid, low-cost, high-throughput and on-line analytical approach is needed at all stages of cereal production and processing in order to guarantee the quality and safety of the production.

To develop the idea to evaluate the potential application of the e-nose technology as an on-line continuous monitoring and controlling tool in cereal processing, a step by step procedure must be designed: knowledge of e-nose characteristics and applications in the cereal industry, proper selection of an appropriate e-nose system for the specific application, analysis of the cereal milling process to identify the optimal points for the e-nose analysis, analyze the critical points for the use of the e-nose in an integrated system for quality evaluation.

II. THE ELECTRONIC NOSE

The e-nose is an instrument which comprises an array of electronic chemical sensors, with partial specificity and an appropriate pattern recognition system, capable of recognizing simple or complex volatile organic compounds' (VOCs) patterns associated to a product odour [3]. The conventional aroma analysis by gas chromatography–mass spectrometry (GC–MS) is too time-consuming, complex and labour-intensive for routine quality application. Compared to GC-MS, e-nose presents several advantages (portable, ease to use, rapid response and low costs) which make it a powerful tool for screening analysis to address the needs for routine quality testing in the food industry. Moreover, it could be easily integrated in current production processes.

Fungal spoilage induces nutritional losses, off-flavours, organoleptic deterioration often associated to mycotoxins formation. Researches have correlated fungal activity with the production of typical VOCs [5]. E-nose technique has been proposed as a new method for the detection of VOCs as indicators of potential grain spoilage, detection and differentiation of mycotoxigenic strains of fungi in contaminated grains and semi-quantitative/quantitative evaluation of mycotoxin contamination [4][5]. This latter has been done using fungal VOCs as indicators of mycotoxin presence. The use of e-nose as a screening tool for the presence of mycotoxins in food must take into accounts the maximum levels or guidance values established by legislation. Preliminary results are encouraging, showing that it is possible to use volatile compounds to predict whether the mycotoxin levels in grains are below or above maximum permitted levels (Figure 1) [6][7].

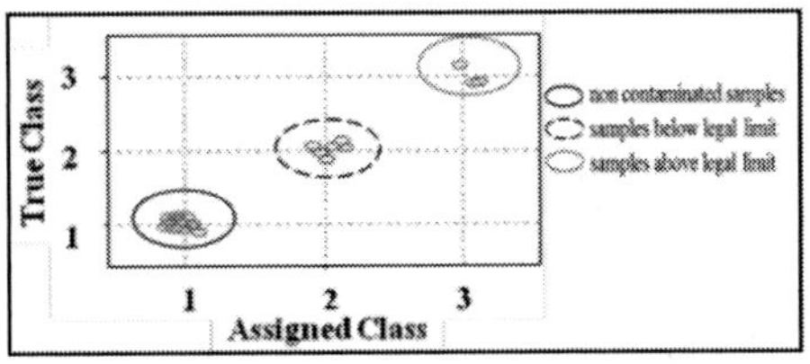

Figure 1. E-nose for the recognition of durum wheat naturally contaminated by deoxynivalenol (CART-model performance plot) (adapted from [8]).

Sampling is the greatest source of error in quantifying mycotoxin contamination because of the difficulty in obtaining samples from large grain consignments and of the uneven distribution of mycotoxins within a commodity [8]. Sampling uncertainty dominates in final uncertainty result, and then the adoption of an on-line e-nose analysis may represent an interesting analytical approach to reduce this uncertainty.

Many characteristics that directly determine the effective quality and/or safety of a food are often described by its aroma. The e-nose is able to provide a global aroma fingerprint, which reflects the aroma complexity of a product. Thus, the evaluation of the "total quality" of food, which requires the simultaneous recognition, classification, and/or quantification of several parameters, could be achieved via a method based on the features and properties exhibited by e-nose. Consequently, e-nose could be applied for both research & development purposes and in-field applications (e.g., in food industry contexts and in production plants).

A. *Set the e-nose for the specific application*

The suitability of an e-nose for a specific application is highly dependent on the required operating conditions (environment) of the sensor array and the composition of the target VOCs. A proper selection of an appropriate e-nose system for a particular application must involve an evaluation on a case-by-case basis. E-nose selection for a particular application must necessarily include: assessments of the selectivity and sensitivity range of individual sensor arrays for particular target VOCs (i.e., related to mycotoxin contamination, target organoleptic properties of the products), the number of unnecessary (redundancy) sensors with similar sensitivities, as well as sensor accuracy, reproducibility, response speed, recovery rate, robustness, and overall performance. Most of these steps are common points of a validation procedure. To set up the e-nose for mycotoxin analysis, naturally contaminated samples will be divided into two subsets. One of the two subsets, training set, will be used to calibrate the model, and the other one, validation set, will be used to verify the robustness of the established model. Pattern recognition systems (principal component analysis - PCA; linear discriminant analysis - LDA) will be employed to select variables and build a model to improve the sample discrimination according to mycotoxin contamination. Results may give crucial information for the development of on-line e-nose devices involving a reduction in sensor number (relative to larger bench-top laboratory instrument versions) and identifying specific sensor types in the array to optimize the performance for specific applications. An important final consideration for designing e-nose systems as a rapid screening tool for food industrial applications is the incidence, frequency and acceptable rate of false classifications. Besides mycotoxin analysis, the set up and validation protocol could be used for enhancing the performance of the sensor system for a "total quality evaluation". New ways to improve e-nose performance using better or more target-specific sensors, pattern-recognition algorithms, data analysis methods, will significantly amplify the range of applications of e-noses in the food industry.

B. *An eye in the cereal milling process for on-line process e-nose analysis*

Food process control necessitates real-time monitoring at critical processing points. Very schematically, the chain of the cereal milling process includes three main steps: receiving and storage of grains, production (milling process) and storage of products and by-products (Figure 2). The dry milling process of wheat is a gradual reduction process by which wheat is ground into flour or semolina, including several steps, such as cleaning and sorting, debranning and milling. At the industrial level, several on-line technological solutions for rapid and non-destructive analysis and quality control of the grain before and after milling are available, such as optical sorters, near infrared (NIR)-based analysis technology, on-line colour, contrast and ash control of cereal products.

The e-nose could be used as an on-line sensing solution at different point (Figure 2): 1) receiving and storing of grain for controlling the safety aspect (i.e., mycotoxin contamination); 2) at the end of the milling process for controlling the quality and safety of the finished product (i.e., organoleptic characteristics, mycotoxin contamination, etc.); 3) after storing before products are packaged or delivered to ensure that they meet specifications according to the specific use. E-nose data may be continuously calculated, transmitted and integrated in the process control system.

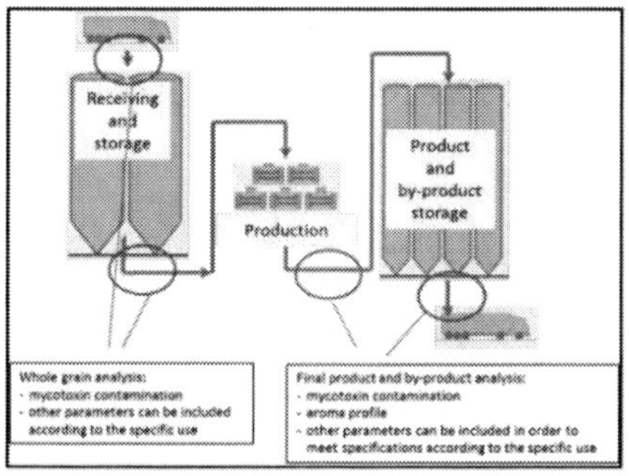

Figure 2. Schematic representation of the chain of the cereal milling process and the possible e-nose optimal points for product and process "total quality" evaluation.

III. E-NOSE IN AN INTEGRATED SYSTEM FOR TOTAL QUALITY EVALUATION

In order to achieve a "total quality evaluation" of cereal products and by-products, e-nose data should be integrated with data from several on-line technological solutions for rapid and non-destructive analysis already are available (like those mentioned before, i.e., optical sorters, NIR-based analysis technology, etc.) to create a technological platform for food process monitoring. Multi-sensor data fusion is a technology able to combine information from several sources in order to improve the monitoring process performance.

Low-level data fusion (direct integration of the raw data of various sensors) and intermediate-level data fusion (data fusion after the feature extraction process to keep enough raw information and eliminate redundant information) will be evaluated for classification efficacy in food quality evaluation. However, the final goal is to create a high-level fusion, namely decision-making fusion, able to analyze the features from each analytical system first and then to associate these features to produce a fused result. For intelligent loops, all the data must be transmitted to the process control system for a continuous quality assurance. Alarm messages must be issued in the case of drift-away from the target value to advice the operators.

IV. CONCLUSION AND FUTURE WORK

E-nose represents a powerful tool for safety and quality evaluation in cereal processing. Despite the advantages of e-nose analysis, there are still few applications of e-nose adopted in industry. This could be attributed to the need to tune either the software and/or hardware to a specific application. Therefore, future work is needed on the materials' side (new material for better selectivity, design and development of sensors that can be used reliably over long temporal horizons), on the data analysis side (better modeling and correlation between chemical markers and the sensor response, development of data fusion analysis for the process control system for a continuous quality assurance), on the industrial side (better understanding of the industrial needs related to quality control and monitoring of food processing).

REFERENCES

[1] C. P. Wild and Y.Y. Gong, "Mycotoxins and human disease: a largely ignored global health issue", Carcinogenesis, vol. 31, Jan. 2010, pp. 71-82, doi: 10.1093/carcin/bgp264.

[2] F. Berthiller et al., "Developments in mycotoxin analysis: an update for 2012-2013", World Mycotoxin Journal, Feb. 2014, vol. 7, pp. 3-33, doi: 10.3920/WMJ2013.1637.

[3] J. W. Gardner and P. N. Bartlett, "A brief history of electronic noses", Sensors Actuators B: Chemical, vol. 18, April 1994, pp 210-211, doi: 10.1016/0925-4005(94)87085-3.

[4] N. Magan and P. Evans, "Volatiles as an indicator of fungal activity and differentiation between species, and the potential use of electronic nose technology for early detection of grain spoilage", Journal of Stored Products Research, vol. 36, Oct. 2000, pp. 319-340, doi: 10.1016/S0022-474X(99)00057-0.

[5] N. Sahgal, R. Needeman, F. J. Cabanes, and N. Magan, "Potential for detection and discrimination between mycotoxigenic and non-toxigenic moulds using volatile production pattern: A review", Food Additives & Contamiants, vol. 24, Oct 2007, pp 1161-1168, doi: 10.1080/02652030701519096.

[6] F. Cheli, A. Campagnoli, L. Pinotti, G. Savoini, and V. Dell'Orto,. "Electronic nose for determination of aflatoxins in maize", Biotechnology, Agronomy, Society and Environment, vol. 13S, 2009, pp. 39-43,

[7] A. Campagnoli et al., "Use of the electronic nose as a screening tool for the recognition of durum wheat naturally contaminated by deoxynivalenol: a preliminary approach", Sensors, vol. 11, May 2011, pp. 4899-4916, doi:10.3390/s110504899.

[8] F. Cheli, A. Campagnoli, L. Pinotti, E. Fusi, and V. Dell'Orto, "Sampling feed for mycotoxins: acquiring knowledge from food" Italian Journal of Animal Science, vol. 8, Jan 2009, pp. 5-22, doi: 10.4081/ijas.2009.5.

Receiver Signal Quality of Ultrasonic Clamp-on Sensors in Dependency on the Transducer Positions

Anett Bailleu
Department 1-Energy and Information
HTW Berlin, University of applied science
Berlin, Germany
e-mail: anett.bailleu@htw-berlin.de

Abstract—**In applications with ultrasonic clamp-on sensors measurement, accuracy and repeatability are significantly worse when compared to ultrasonic inline sensors in spite of both sensor types using the same measurement principle. The positioning of the ultrasonic transducers of clamp-on sensors has a determining influence on the precision and accuracy of the measurement results. A study was made of sound propagation and receiver signal quality as they vary depending on the distance between the ultrasonic transmitter and the ultrasonic receiver. As a result of studying transducer sensitivity, it was possible to implement an automatic positioning system for ultrasonic clamp-on sensor applications. The positioning system automatically finds an optimal transducer position for a particular application. This allows the user to operate a clamp-on sensor without having any special knowledge of the application procedure or needing to set any parameters of the system in advance.**

Keywords—ultrasonic clamp-on sensor; receiver signal quality; propagation of sound; transducer positioning

I. Introduction

Today, a well-known application area for ultrasonic clamp-on sensors is in the flowmeters which are used in many industrial processes [1-6] .

Ultrasonic clamp-on sensors offer the opportunity to measure other parameters, for example density and the concentration of ingredients in fluids [7-10] .

Other kinds of ultrasonic clamp-on sensors allow detection of the composition of homogenous alloys or can distinguish synthetic materials without any chemical analysis [11]. Such systems are used where non-destructive material control is required.

A. *State of the Art*

The main advantage of all these kinds of ultrasonic clamp-on measurements is the possibility to measure non-invasively. Parameters can be detected offline or online, so one does not have to disconnect a running system. This advantage led to successful development and deployment of clamp-on transducers for more than twenty-five years [12].

There are also some disadvantages of using ultrasonic clamp-on sensors particularly in comparison to ultrasonic sensors with fixed-mounted transducers in a complete sensor system. The main functional components, transducers and electronics of these different ultrasonic sensors generally operate in the same way. Only the positioning of the transducers is significantly different [13]. The greatest signal amplitudes and the best signal to noise ratio are expected when the transmitter and the receiver are located in an optimal relative position.

Thus, the proposal is the following: if the positioning of the ultrasonic transducers can be optimized, then the precision of the measuring in clamp-on applications is improved.

B. *Aim of the Study*

This study concentrates on flowmeter applications and finding an optimal relative position between an ultrasonic transmitter and an ultrasonic receiver when placed on a water-filled pipe. Without the influence of any flow, the signal quality of the receiver was measured as solely dependent on the distance between the transducers. The maximum amplitude for the envelope curve of the receiver signal is a sure indicator of an optimal distance between transmitter and receiver. An automatic transducer positioning system for clamp-on flowmeter applications was developed using this criterion.

C. *Structure of the Paper*

The paper is subdivided into five main sections. According to this instruction, some relevant theoretical basics are elucidated and illustrated in section 'Theory'. The section 'Measurements' contains a description of the experimental setup, the measurement results and an interpretation of the represented series of receiver signals. In section 'Development of an Automatic Transducer Positioning System', such a system for clamp-on ultrasonic transducers is briefly depicted. In a last section, a summary and an outlook are written.

II. Theory

One of these optimal relative positions results from the v-, and w-model arrangements of the transducers. The basis of these model arrangements is the Snellius-law of reflection. It describes the change of the direction of propagation at boundaries between media with different sound velocities [14].

The sound propagation between an ultrasonic transmitter and an ultrasonic receiver (see Figures 1 and 2) takes place by Rayleigh waves (surface acoustic waves) and by transversal and longitudinal waves.

Furthermore, as is generally known, ultrasonic sound velocity depends on material properties [15]. In solids, the ultrasonic sound propagation is a result of volumetric deformation and shear deformation. All kinds of waves propagate in solid materials like the wall of the pipe. The sound velocity depends on the bulk modulus, the shear modulus and the density of the material in which the ultrasonic wave is travelling. Fluids do not transmit shear forces therefore only longitudinal waves have the capability to spread in liquids and gases. Typically, longitudinal waves travel faster in materials than do transversal waves [16]. Furthermore, the sound velocity of Rayleigh waves is less than the sound velocity of transversal waves [17].

$$c_{RAYLEIGH} < c_{transversal} < c_{longitudinal} \,. \quad (1)$$

Figure 1 depicts the relevant distances, the inclination angle α, the shortest path of surface acoustic waves (Rayleigh waves) and the path of reflective waves at the wall of the pipe.

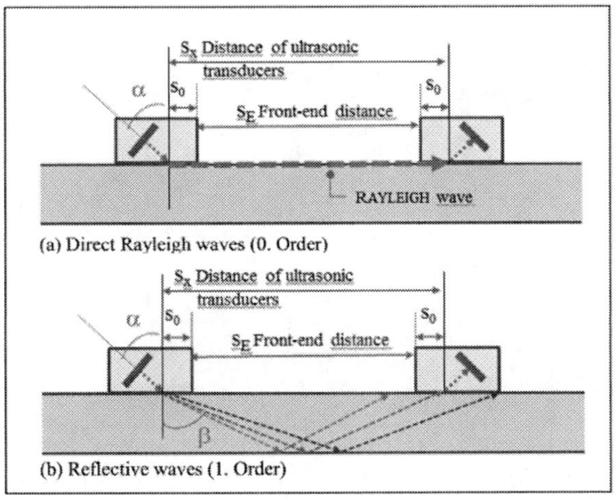

Figure 1. Paths of ultrasonic waves at the wall of the pipe

Another aspect of sound propagation is the superposition of different orders in the pipe through the fluid (Figure 2).

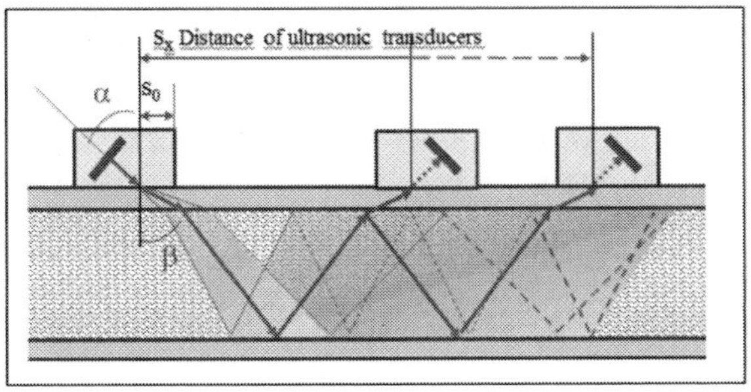

Figure 2. Sound propagation with beam spread instead of supersonic jets

A widespread beam is really propagated instead of a supersonic jet. Such a widespread beam has a similar effect like an instability or uncertainty of the inclination angle.

Both the breadth of the real beam spread and the superposition of multiple reflections constitute reasons why there is a measurement effect in nearly every distance between the ultrasonic transmitter and receiver (Figure 2).

III. Measurements

A. *General Description of the Experimental Setup*

The experimental setup is shown in Figures 3 to 6. Each horizontal pipe (Figure 3) consists of a different material. The pipes are filled with water. Ultrasonic clamp-on transducers can be mounted on these pipes. Usually, this is achieved by pipe clamps such as those used by the transducers of the reference clamp-on flowmeter F601 from the Flexim GmbH company (Figure 3a). Figure 3 shows the main parts of the experimental setup.

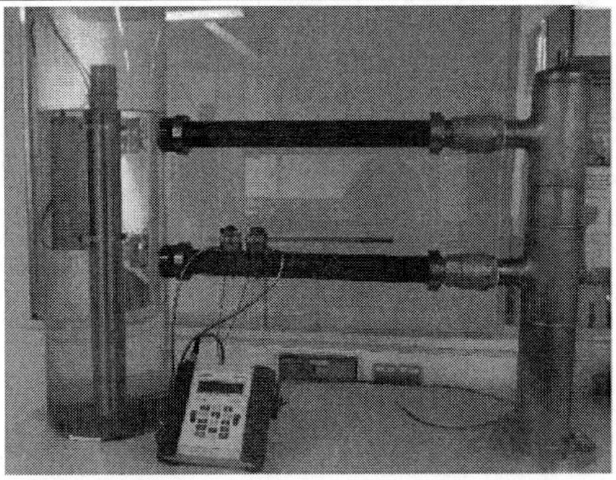

(a) Photographic image

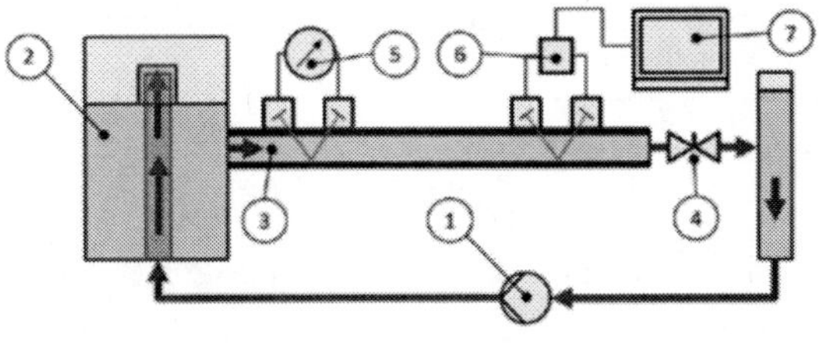

(b) Schematic drawing [18]

Figure 3. Setup with water filled pipes for testing ultrasonic clamp-on sensors

The experimental setup (Figure 3b) consists of:

- (1) A pump
- (2) A cylindric fluid reservoir
- (3) Two pipes with a flowing fluid (water)
  - The upper one consists of pertinax.
  - The lower one consists of steel

- (4) A valve (manual adjustability)
- (5) A reference clamp-on flowmeter (F601 from the Flexim GmbH company)
- (6) A test clamp-on system
- (7) Oscilloscope (DSO) PM or PC with ADC

In the test case, a pair of ultrasonic clamp-on transducers was mounted with only the force of permanent magnets on a pipe of steel (Figure 4). This made it very simple to change the distance between the transducers in the test scenario.

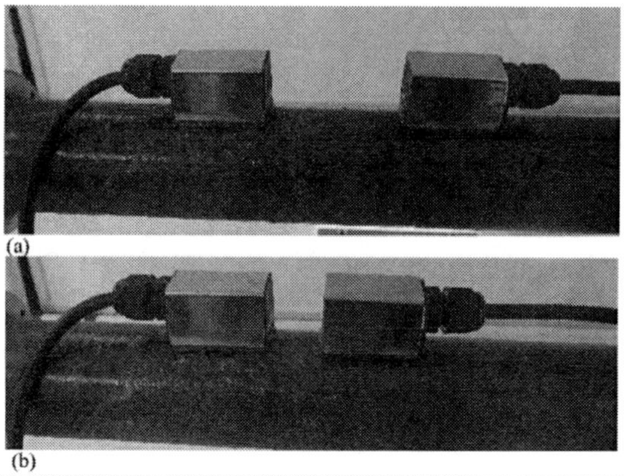

Figure 4. A pair of magnetic ultrasonic clamp-on sensors on a pipe of rusty steel mounted at different distances

To study how the received signal quality depends on the distance between the transducers, the distance between the front-ends of the housings of the ultrasonic transmitter and the ultrasonic receiver was measured. The front-end distance of the housings is smaller than the real transducer distance. The relationship between the distances is illustrated in Figures 1 and 5. Ultrasonic transducers of a TUF2000-Clamp-on flowmeter were used for the experiments (Figures 4 and 5). In Figure 5 the pipe-sided design of the transducers used is photographed.

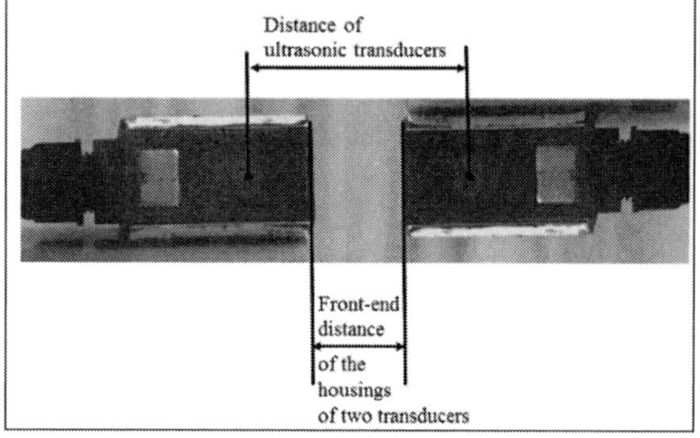

Figure 5. Distance between the ultrasonic transducers

B. *Technical Specifications*

The experimental setup used in the presented studies of ultrasonic signal quality considered paths without any flow (v=0 m/s). So, it was not necessary to use the installed clamp-on reference flowmeter (F601) for the presented studies.

The main parameters of the experimental setup are:

- The outer diameter of the used steel pipe: 60 mm.
- The thickness of wall of the pipe: 2±0,1mm.
- The distance of ultrasonic transducers:

$$s_{TR} = s_E + 2*s_0 \; ; \qquad (2)$$

(s_E = Front-end distance s_0 = 12 mm [18]).

The ultrasonic transmitter is driven by an electronic burst generator. Every burst consists of 10 single pulses. While the frequency of the burst sequence is 1 kHz, the frequency of the single pulses in the bursts is about 1 MHz. The signals of the transmitter and the receiver were observed with an oscilloscope (DSO PM3394, 200 MHz, 200 MS/s, 16 bit ADC). In the detected signals of the receiver the transmitting burst is also observed (Figure 6). This is a helpful effect of electromagnetic crosstalk (see below).

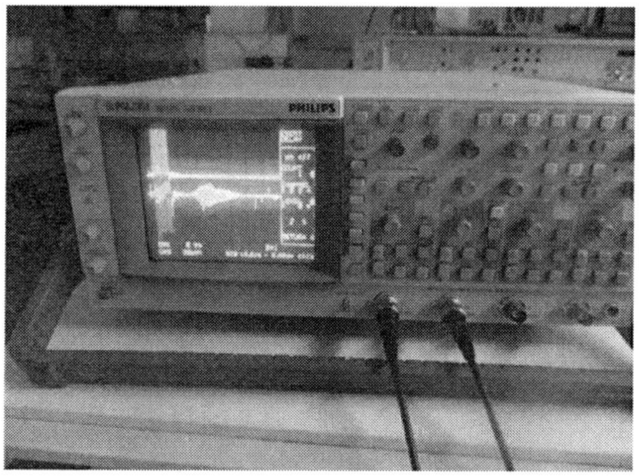

Figure 6. Typical visualization of the transmitter and the receiver signal with electromagnetic crosstalk

C. *Signal Interpretation*

The observed parasitic crosstalk is helpful to detect absolute transmitting times of the ultrasonic signal passing the distance between the transmitter and the receiver by analyzing the data of only one channel. For instance, a representative measurement series of signals of the receiver channel dependend on the distance of the ultrasonic transducers is printed in Figure 7 (Ultrasonic transducer distance s_{TR} =: front-end distance value s_E + 24 mm):

$$s_{TR} = s_E + 2*12 \text{ mm}. \qquad (3)$$

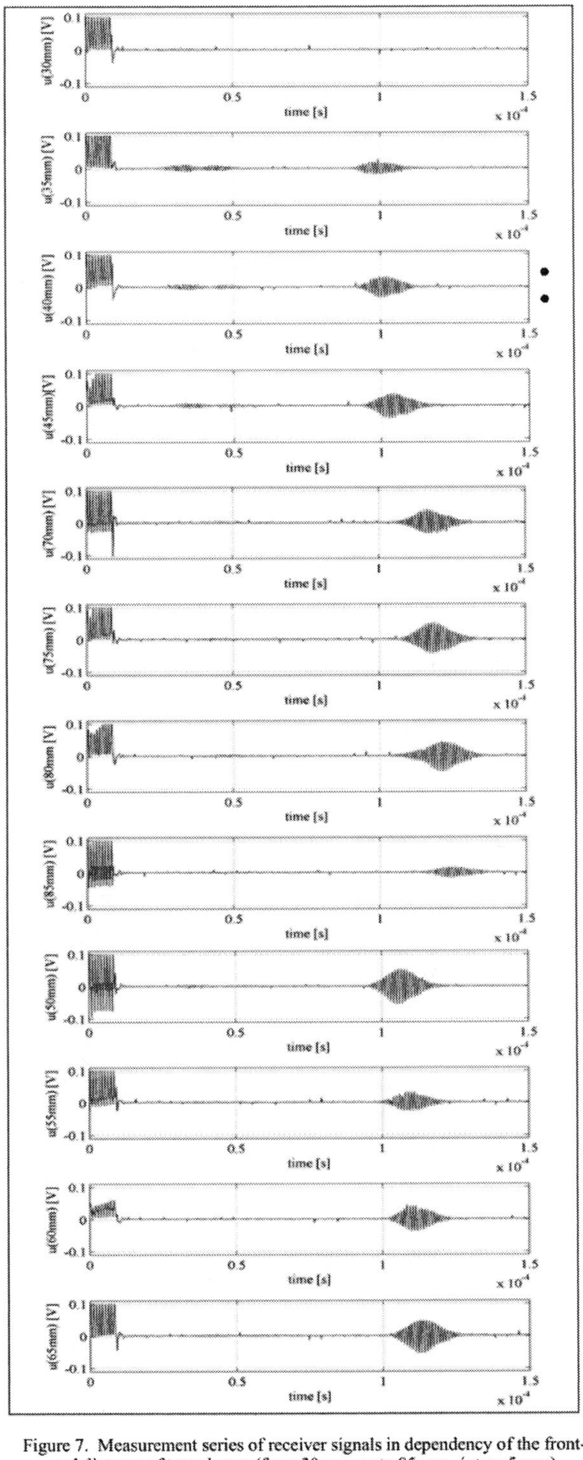

Figure 7. Measurement series of receiver signals in dependency of the front-end distance of transducers (from 30 mm up to 85 mm / step: 5 mm)

A significant correlation between the transit time and the transducer distance is shown. The relevant time slot of the receiver signal can be easily observed.

Furthermore, the experiment indicates that the amplitude of the receiver signal does not decrease with the distance of the transducers.

Constructive and destructive interferences seem to have the effect of periodical increasing and decreasing of the envelope curve of the receiver signal.

In this case, the best signal noise ratios are found to be:

- $s_{TR\_1} = s_{E\_50} + 24$ mm = (50+24) mm = 74 mm,
- $s_{TR\_2} = s_{E\_65} + 24$ mm = (65+24) mm = 89 mm.

Such studies will be continued by using a novel automatic transducer positioning system.

IV. Development of an Automatic Transducer Positioning System

Following evaluation of experiments and some theoretical studies an automatic transducer positioning system for clamp-on sensors was developed and implemented [19]. This positioning system (Figures 8 and 9) consists of a motorized linear track. The system is augmented with sensors to detect the temperature, the pipe outer diameter and the pipe wall thickness. This makes a complete, generic measurement system for pipes.

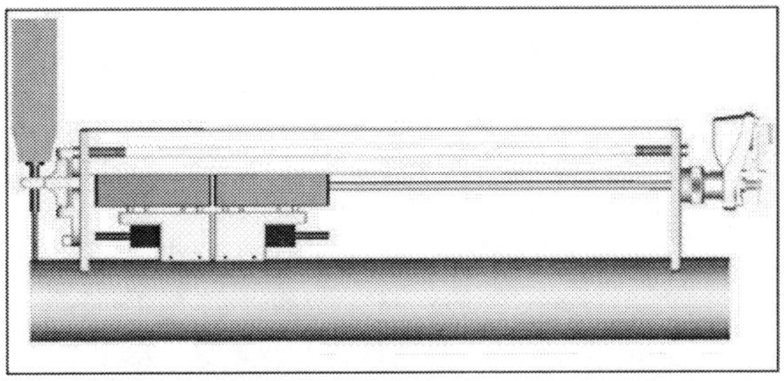

Figure 8. Construction of the positioning system [19]

The system is augmented with sensors to detect the temperature, the pipe outer diameter and the pipe wall thickness. This makes a complete, generic measurement system for pipes.

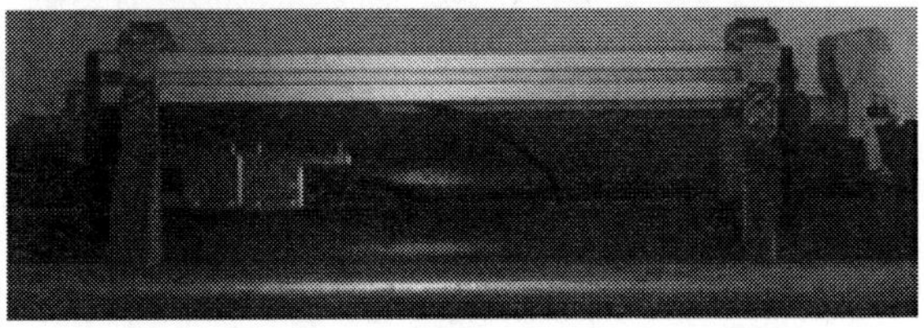

Figure 9. Photographic image of the positioning system [19]

Only one of the pair of transducers is moved by the system. A stepper motor is used for this functionality.

V. Summary and Outlook

A study was made of signal quality and the resulting signal noise ratio dependent on the distance between the transducers. During the study, a system was created which automatically detects all relevant parameters to set the optimal distance between the ultrasonic clamp-on transducers in a particular application [19].

Including further variables would require additional sensors in this solution, for example sound velocities, temperature or geometric parameters of the pipe. But it seems possible to measure the effect of all relevant parameters with the required accuracy by varying the position of the pair of ultrasonic transducers. By motorized motion of one transducer the ultrasound path between the transmitter and the receiver can be varied optimally for different measurement tasks.

Acknowledgments

The implementation of the transducer positioning system was supported by Kieback & Peter GmbH. The experimental setup was sponsored by Flexim GmbH.

I would like to thank the students S. Schacht and S. Brych for their practical implementation of measurements and our fruitful discussions.

References

[1] F. Cascetta, "Application of a portable clamp-on ultrasonic flowmeter in the water industry," in Flow Measurement and Instrumentation, vol. 5, pp. 191-194, July 1994, doi:10.1016/science.09555986(94)90019-1

[2] J. M. Szebeszczy, "Application of clamp-on ultrasonic flowmeter for industrial flow measurements," in Flow Measurement and Instrumentation, vol. 5, pp. 127-131, April 1994, doi:10.1016/science.09555986(94)90047-7

[3] B. Svensson and J. Delsing, "Application of ultrasonic clamp-on flow meters for in situ tests of billing meters in district heating systems," in Flow Measurement and Instrumentation, vol. 9, pp. 33-41, Jan 1998, doi:10.1016/science.0955-5986(98)00007-7

[4] Siemens: Nuclear-PICS-00093-0514.pdf, [Online]. Available from: http://www.industry.usa.siemens.com/automation/us/en /process-instrumentation-and-analytics/processinstrumen-tation/ flow -measurement/ ultrasonic-clamp-on/ 2015.11.30

[5] Siemens: E20001-A60-P730-V1-7600.pdf, [Online].Available from: http://www.industry.usa.siemens.com/automation/us/en /process-instrumentation-and-analytics/processinstrumen-tation/ flow -measurement/ ultrasonic-clamp-on/ 2015.11.30

[6] GE: gc868_brochure_english_0.pdf, [Online]. Available from: https://www.gemeasurement.com/sites/gemc.dev/files/ 2015.11.30

[7] P. Hauptmann, B. Henning, R. Lucklum and A. Zuber,"Ultrasonic system for industrial process data acuisition in fluids, in tm-Technisches Messen, vol. 59 (1992), pp. 63-68

[8] B. Henning, R. Lucklum, B. Kupfernagel and P. Hauptmann, "Ultrasonic sensor system for characterization of liquid systems" in Sensors and Actuators A, 41-42 (1994), pp. 476 - 480.

[9] A. Püttmer, P. Hauptmann, B. Henning and R. Lucklum, "Ultrasonic sensor system for dairy industry," Sensors Series. ed. by A.T.Augousti. in "Sensors and their Applications VII". Institute of Physics Publishing (UK). (1995), pp. 141 - 145.

[10] Smerdin, S.; Doerner, S.; Schönfelder, G.; Hauptmann, P.: The Ultrasonic Sensor System for Measurement of Density of Liquids. XIII Session of the Russian Acoustical Society, Moscow, August 25-29, 2003, pp. 443 – 446.

[11] M. Berke, "Nondestructive material testing with ultrasonics. Introduction to the basic principles," in NDT.net, vol. 5 (09) 2000, [Online]. Available from: http://www.ndt.net/article /v05n09/berke/berke1.htm

[12] Flexim: We set standards, [Online]. Available from: http://www.flexim.com/us/flexim/when-measuring-matters/2015.10.02

[13] O. Keitmann-Curdes and B. Funck , "A new calibration method for ultrasonic clamp-on transducers", in Proceedings of the IEEE Ultrasonics Symposium, pp. 517-520, · January 2008, doi: 10.1109/ULTSYM.2008.0125

[14] Tribikram Kundu (Editor), "Ultrasonic and Electromagnetic NDE for Structure and Material Characterization," CRC Press, Boca Raton FL, 2012, pp.42-56, ISBN 978-1-439-83663-7, S. 42–56

[15] J. Krautkrämer and H. Krautkrämer, "Ultrasonic testing of materials", 4th ed. ,1990 , Springer-Verlag, Berlin, ISBN 978-3-540-51231-8.

[16] R. Millner, "Ultraschalltechnik-Grundlagen und Anwend-ungen," p.27, Physik-Verlag, Germany 1987

[17] L. N. Maurer,_ S. Mei, and I. Knezevic, "Rayleigh surface waves and phonon mode conversion in nanostructures," (Dated: 2016/03/02) [Online]. Available from: http://arxiv.org/pdf/1510.01637 / 2016/03/09

[18] S. Brych, "Untersuchung der Signalauswertung einer Lauf-zeitdifferenzmessung in der Clamp-on-Ultraschall-technologie", bachelor thesis, 2015, unpublished.

[19] S. Schacht, "Entwicklung eines Einmessverfahrens mit auto-matischer Positioniereinheit in der Ultraschall Clamp-On-Technologie", master thesis, 2015, unpublished.

A Room Temperature Operated Carbon Dioxide Sensor Based on EB-PANI/ PEDOT:PSS Sensing Material

Yu-Cheng Su
Graduate Institute of Electronics Engineering
National Taiwan University
Taipei, Taiwan
e-mail: r030943066@ntu.edu.tw

Chih-Ting Lin
Graduate Institute of Electronics Engineering
National Taiwan University
Taipei, Taiwan
e-mail: timlin@cc.ee.ntu.edu.tw

Wen-Yu Chung
Graduate Institute of Electronics Engineering
National Taiwan University
Taipei, Taiwan
e-mail: d99943047@ntu.edu.tw

Wen-Jong Wu
Department of Engineering Science and Ocean Engineering
National Taiwan University
Taipei, Taiwan
e-mail: jrywu@ntumems.net

***Abstract*—To resolve the high power consumption and complex polymerization process of most CO_2 sensors, a room temperature operation CO_2 sensor based on Emeraldine base – polyaniline (EB-PANI) blended with poly(3,4-ethylenedioxythiophene) polystyrene sulfonate (PEDOT:PSS) was developed. In this work, the sensor performed linear response to CO_2 in working range of 1000-20000 ppm with the response from 0.98% to 3.83%. This detection range is low enough for environmental detection. On the other hand, compared to the response to CO_2, this sensor has considerably lower response to humidity, from 50 % to 85 % RH. Hence, in the ambient environment, this CO_2 sensor is not affected by humidity when detecting the CO_2 concentration.**

Keywords-CO_2 sensor; polyaniline; PEDOT:PSS.

I. INTRODUCTION

CO_2 is a common gas in our life and plays an important role for agriculture [1], indoor air quality [2], food storage [3], etc. For indoor air quality, the safe CO2 concentration rage is between 1500 ppm and 5000 ppm. A higher concentration would lead to people feeling sleepy, having headaches, inattention [2] and so on. Furthermore, it has been proven that, by integrating a CO_2 sensor into the ventilation system, the ventilating strength level can be adjusted depending on the CO_2 concentration. This makes the ventilation system more efficient and can reduce about 10%~30% of energy consumption and ventilation loads [4]. On the other hand, in health care, a CO_2 sensor can be used to monitor patients respiratory capacity, and, hence, lung condition. The general standard is from 4% to 6%, or the patient might be under the risk of metabolic acidosis or respiratory failure.

Based on these important applications, many researchers developed various new sensing materials for CO_2 sensing, such as copper oxide and spinel ferrite nanocomposite [5], $LaFeO_3$ [6] and other metal oxide of nanocomposite [7]. However, metal oxide based sensors need to operate at high temperature, which are from 150°C to 300°C, and this requires a large energy consumption. Therefore, other research works focus on polymer-based materials to avoid this problem, such as PEDOT [8], RGO [9], and PANI [10]. However, the chemical inertness of carbon dioxide has caused many difficulties in developing polymer base CO_2 chemical sensors [11]. For example, RGO sensor needs high voltage plasma treatment to recover the sensing feature after measurement [9]; SPAN sensor's detection limit is too high (20000ppm) and the polymerization process is complicated [12][13]; PEDOT and PANI sensors need to detect CO_2 with high humidity to improve the sensitivity [8][10]. Therefore, for environmental CO_2 detection, these problems still need to improve.

In this work, Emeraldine base–polyaniline (EB-PANI) blended with poly(3,4-ethylenedioxythiophene) polystyrene sulfonate (PEDOT:PSS) was used to be a sensing film. In Oleg P Dimitriev ed. Al. study [14], the authors claimed that the blending of PEDOT:PSS can improve PANI's conductivity because of PSS's co-doping in PEDOT and EB-PANI. According to previous research, it was expected that the blending of PEDOT:PSS can also increase the water absorption ability compared to pure EB-PANI and then increase bicarbonate formation [15]. Furthermore, it was also expected that the PSS co-doping will cause the sulfonic acid polyaniline (SPAN). Based on the assumption, EB-PANI/PEDOT:PSS would be an appropriate sensing material for indoor CO_2 monitoring.

The remainder of this paper is structured as follows. In Section II, the fabrication process and measurement steps are described. In Section III, the sensing result and the humidity effect are discussed. We conclude in Section IV.

II. EXPERIMENT AND MEASUREMENT

This experiment is composed of two parts, one is the fabrication process of sensing film and substrate; the other is measurement system set-up and method.

A. Sensor fabrication

A p-type wafer with 300 nm oxide on the top of surface was used as the device substrate. The substrate was cleaned by acetone and isopropyl alcohol. After that, the substrate was dry out by heating and N_2 gas to remove humidity. This was followed by photolithography. The electrode was defined with W/L in the ratio of 800 um/40 um. Then, the sensing electrodes, i.e., 20 nm/200 nm of Cr/Au electrodes, were achieved by e-gun evaporation and lift-off process.

First, EB-PANI powder was dissolved in N-methylpyrrolidinone (NMP) to prepare a stock solution with concentration of 1 wt.%. Then, 1 w.t.% of PEDOT:PSS aqueous solution was added slowly into 1 w.t.% of EB-PANI solution in 1:1 proportion (v/v). After adding materials into solutions, the blended solution was mixing well by stirring. Finally, the sensing film was fabricating by drop-casting, and baking in dynamic vacuum for 24hr in 60°C. Figure 1 shows the structure of EB-PANI and PEDOT:PSS. In our assumption, this mixing will make the EB-PANI reform to Sulfonic Acid polyaniline (SPAN), which will change the working range for environmental monitoring [12].

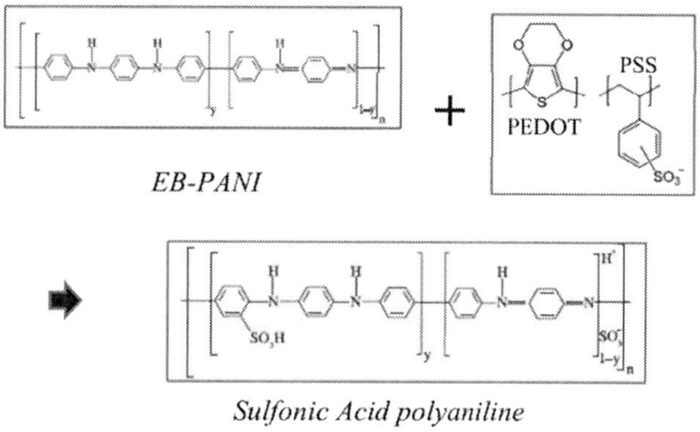

Figure 1. Structure of sensing material: EB-PANI and PEDOT:PSS, and SPAN.

B. Measurement system

To measure the response of the developed sensing material, the LCR meter, Agilent E4980A, provides DC 1V to measure the resistance of the sensing film. Figure 2 shows the measurement system. The gas sensing experiment was operated in the chamber. Before gas sensing, the chamber was vacuumed by a mechanical pump for 5 minutes to remove the ambient gas; the vacuum level was below 0.2 torr. After that, the dry air (79% N_2 and 21% O_2) was flown into the chamber for 3 minutes, then, the vacuum process was repeated. After removing dry air by vacuuming for 5 minutes, CO_2 with dry air was then flown into the chamber and, next, we waited for 5 minutes.

In order to simulate the real life environment, CO_2 detection was measured in various relative humidity conditions. Therefore, Deionized water (DI water) was ink-jeted and flown in with dry air and CO_2. The water fully vaporizes. The relative humidity concentration was detected from a commercial humidity meter. All the measurements were carried out at room temperature.

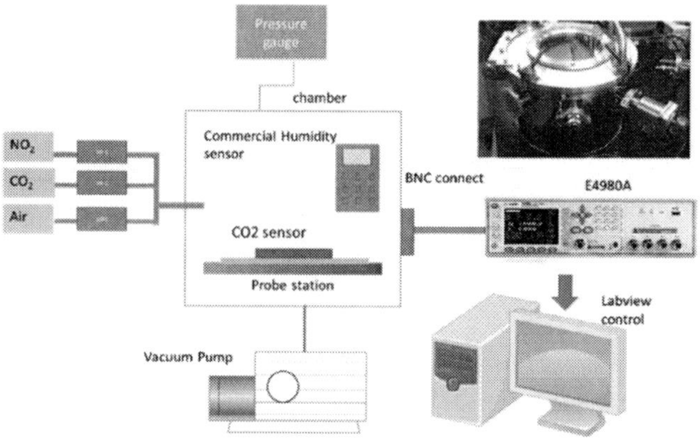

Figure 2. The schematic diagram for gas sensor measurement

The CO_2 concentration in chamber was controlled by Micro Fluid controller (MFC). 500 ppm CO_2 (background is dry air) is a reference gas, then CO_2 and dry air flow rate were controlled to adjust the CO_2 concentration. Each concentration of CO_2 with different humidity was staying in chamber for 3 minutes then removed by vacuum. During measurement, the pressure in the chamber was controlled to be the same as the ambient pressure. Finally, the measured data was recorded by a LabView program.

III. RESULTS AND DISCUSSION

In the following, CO_2 sensitivity and humidity effects are discussed separately.

A. Gas sensing properties

In the case of CO_2 sensing mechanism, Tsuyoshi Tonosaki ed al. [16] claimed that the hydrolysis of CO2 will generate bicarbonate ions, and be incorporated to EB-PANI, which will then become emeraldine salt-PANI (ES-PANI). The ES- PANI is more conductive than EB-PANI. Therefore, the higher CO_2 concentration, the more bicarbonate ions will be generated and cause the EB-PANI transforming into ES type, resulting in the decreasing of the sensing material resistance.

Based on the theory, the response is defined as the following equation:

$$\text{response }(\%) = \frac{R_0 - R_{CO2}}{R_0} \times 100\%$$

where R_0 represents the resistance of sensor in the reference gas. Since the resistance decreased with the rising of CO_2 concentration, the sensitivity can be defined. For a normal indoor ambient environment, the CO_2 concentration is around 500 ppm and humidity is between 65% RH and 75% RH. Therefore, in our measurement, we kept the humidity in this range and 500 ppm CO2 was assumed as the reference gas.

Figure 3 shows the resistance of EB-PANI/PEDOT:PSS sensor decreases when a higher concentration of CO_2 with flow in (with vaporized water). As the CO_2 concentration increases, the resistance decrease, so we can clearly distinguish different concentration of CO_2. The details of the resistance variation are shown in Table 1. In this table, the response time can be observed, which is around 40 seconds and the recovery time is around 250 seconds. Figure 4 is the sensor response to different CO_2 concentrations, which are from 1000 ppm to 50000 ppm. The result shows that the maximum response is at 20000 ppm with response of 3.83%. The linear working range is between 1000 and 20000 ppm. As CO_2 concentration is higher than 20000 ppm, the response will saturate. For environment CO_2 detection, this working range is appropriate for indoor environmental monitoring.

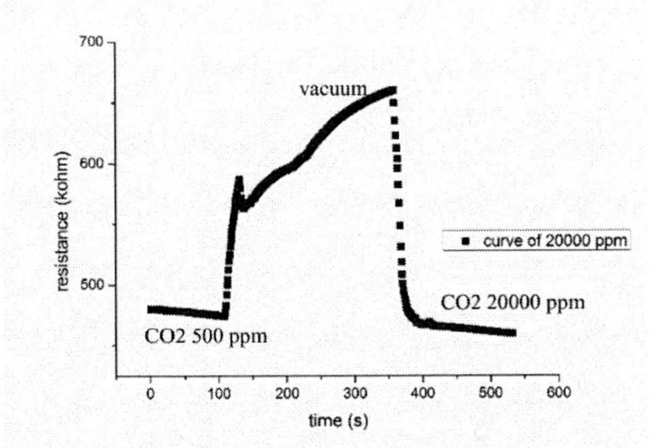

Figure 3. CO_2 response curve of EB-PANI/PEDOT:PSS sensor in humid environment, the humidity was controlled at 70±5% RH. The step of single concentration response measurement is: 1) flow the 500 ppm CO_2 in RH 70%, 2) vacuum the chamber 3) flow the 20000 ppm CO_2 in RH 70%, too.

TABLE I. RESISTANCE VALUE IN FIGURE 3.

CO2 concentration (ppm)	Resistance(Ω)	response
500	477.4k	
20000	462.0k	-3.21%

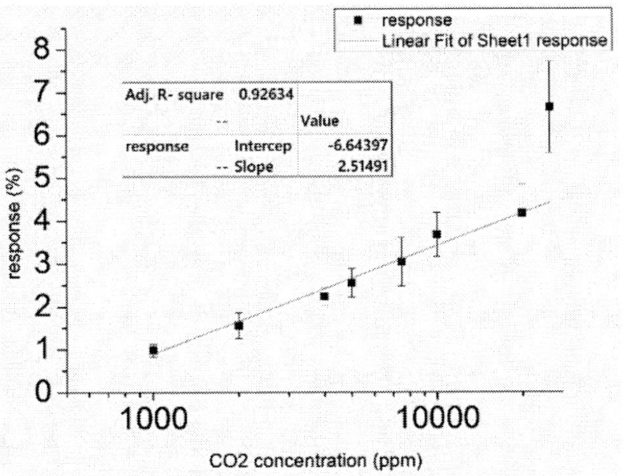

Figure 4. CO_2 response from 1000 to 50000 ppm, which humidity is controlled at 70±5% RH.

B. Humidity effect

For past CO_2 polymer base sensors, most of them significantly depend on the humidity value and need to detect CO_2 with high humidity concentration. However, compared to CO_2 sensitivity, these sensing films showed much higher sensitivity to humidity. To resolve this problem, the hydrophilic material, PEDOT:PSS, was blended into EB-PANI. With this method, it can improve the formation of bicarbonate to enhance CO_2 detection, but improve the selectivity to humidity. Due to the opposing conductivity variation trend of PEDOT:PSS and PANI, in summation the response to humidity was assumed to offset each other then become stable.

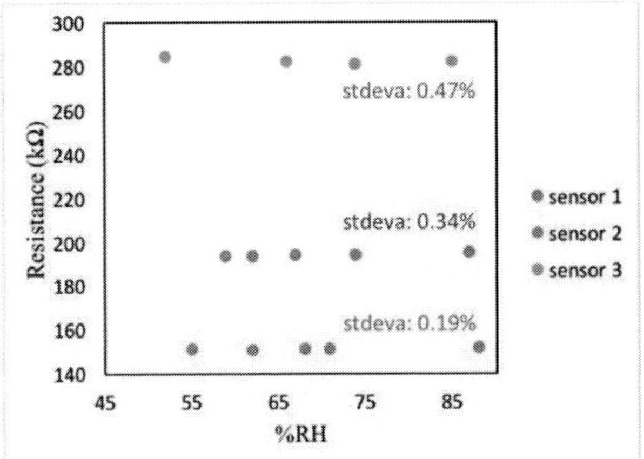

Therefore, the humidity effect is shown in Figure 5. The sensor responses to humidity from 50% RH to 85% RH are much smaller compared to CO_2 response, and there is also no obviously trend of humidity effect. Hence, in ambient environment, this CO_2 sensor can ignore the humidity effect to detect CO_2 concentration. Differences in the original resistance of every sensor would due to process variations, such as blending quality, and the relation of standard variation and resistance still need to be studied.

IV. CONCLUSION

In this paper, a room temperature operated CO_2 sensor has been developed with a simple fabrication process. The detection range is from 1000 ppm to 20000 ppm with highly response from 0.98% to 3.83%. It is appropriate for environmental CO_2 detection. Furthermore, the humidity effect is also discussed. Compared to CO_2 sensitivity, this sensor has extremely low response for humidity. Hence, the blending of PEDOT:PSS into EB-PANI is successfully resolving the problem of humidity effect for most polymer based materials. This CO_2 sensor is highly potential for indoor environmental detection.

ACKNOWLEDGMENT

This work is supported by Ministry of Science and Technology, Taiwan (no.103-2119-M-002-028) and Intel-NTU Connected Context Computing Center (NSC 101-2628-E-002 -022 -MY3, 100-2911-I-002-001, and 101R7501). Also thanks to Material and Chemical Research Laboratories of ITRI for providing nanoparticle samples.

REFERENCES

[1] S.H. Wittwer, "Carbon dioxide and crop productivity," New Scientist 95 (1982): 233-234.

[2] W. Bihlmayr, "CO_2 sensor Design concept for solar-powered CO_2 sensor", APPLICATION NOTE vol. 313, 2011, pp.1-2

[3] A. T. Hagan, "Carbon Dioxide and Nitrogen", Captain Dave, Inc.. retrieved from http://captaindaves.com/foodfaq/the-food-storage-faq-version-4-0/chapter-3-food-storage-containers/carbon-dioxide-and-nitrogen/ [retrieved: March, 2016]

[4] M. Stucky, Senior Content Developer & LEED Green Associate, KMC Controls, (2016, January 19) "Demand Control Ventilation Benefits for Your Building" Retrieved from http://www.realcomm.com/advisory/advisory.asp?AdvisoryID=676 [retrieved: March, 2016]

[5] A. Chapelle, O.H. Fahd, P.Lionel, B. Antoine, and Tailhades, "CO2 sensing properties of semiconducting copper oxide and spinel ferrite nanocomposite thin film," Applied Surface Science, vol. 256 , 2010, pp. 4715-4519. ISSN 0169-4332

[6] X. F. Wang, H. W. Qin , L. H. Sun, and J. F. Hu, "CO2 sensing properties and mechanism of nanocrystalline LaFeO3 sensor," Sensors and Actuators B, vol. 188, 2013, pp. 965–971

[7] R.P. Tandon, M.R. Tripathy, A.K. Arora, and S. Hotchandani, "Gas and humidity response of iron oxide—Polypyrrole nanocomposites," Sensors and Actuators B, vol. 114, 2006, pp. 768–773

[8] B. Andò et al. , "An Inkjet Printed CO2 Gas Sensor" Procedia Engineering, vol.120, 2015, pp. 628 – 631

[9] S. M. Hafiz et al. , "A practical carbon dioxide gas sensor using room-temperaturehydrogen plasma reduced graphene oxide" , Sensors and Actuators B, vol. 193 , 2014, pp. 692–700

[10] K. Ogura, and H. Shiigi," A CO2 Sensing Composite Film Consisting of Base-Type Polyaniline and Poly(vinyl alcohol)", Electrochemical and Solid-State Letters, vol. 2-9, 1999, pp. 478-480

[11] C. J. Chiang et al. , "In situ fabrication of conducting polymer composite film as a chemical resistive CO2 gas sensor" Microelectronic Engineering, vol. 111, 2013, pp. 409–415

[12] T. C.D. Doan et al. , "Carbon dioxide sensing with sulfonated polyaniline", Sensors and Actuators B, vol. 168, 2012, pp. 123–130

[13] S. A. Chen and G. W. Hwang, "Structure Characterization of Self-Acid-Doped Sulfonic Acid Ring-Substituted Polyaniline in Its Aqueous Solutions and as Solid Film," Macromolecules, vol. 29, 1996, pp. 3950-3955

[14] O. P. Dimitriev, "Cooperative doping in polyanilinepoly(ethylene-3,4-dioxythiophene):Poly(styrenesulfonic acid) composite system,"journal of polymer research, vol. 18, 2011, pp. 2435–2440.

[15] X. Crispin et al. , "Conductivity, Morphology, Interfacial Chemistry, and Stability of Poly(3,4-ethylene dioxythiophene)–Poly(styrenesulfonate): A Photoelectron Spectroscopy Study," Journal of Polymer Science: Part B: Polymer Physics, vol. 41, 2003, pp. 2561–2583

[16] T. Tonosaki, T. Oho, H. Shiigi, K. Isomura, and K. Ogura, "Highly Sensitive CO2 Sensor with Polymer Composites Operating at Room Temperature, " ANALYTICAL SCIENCES, vol. 17, 2001, pp. 249-252

Identification of Stress Situations in Urban Space

When biosensors capture emotions

Sana Layeb, Faten Hussein
Research Team on Ambiances,
Graduate School of Architecture and Urbanism
ERA, ENAU
Tunis, Tunisia
E-mails : sana.layeb@yahoo.fr, faten.hussein@gmail.com

Raja Ghozi, Meriem Jaidane
Research Unit on Systems and Signals,
National School of Engineering
U2S, ENIT
Tunis, Tunisia
E-mails: raja.ghozi@ieee.org, meriem.jaidane@planet.tn

***Abstract*—This study raises the question of stress situations in public space. Interested in the well-being of city users while evolving in town, we performed an experimentation based on a multidisciplinary methodology that combines qualitative and quantitative data resulted from commented walks in urban areas at city-center of Tunis. Stress level physiological measurements, called Electro Dermal Activity (EDA), are generated while crossing these areas and analysis of the soundscape were conducted. The target of this paper is to check the links between urban sound phenomenon, the stress of participants and architectural and urban characteristics of space. Our research aims to reduce those stress situations and to propose adequate urban configuration to make the city accessible to everybody.**

Keywords-stress situations; urban space; Electro Dermal Activity ; Q sensor; emotions.

I. INTRODUCTION

Using urban space often calls for physical and perceptive skills [1]. Users experience the city by walking, driving, using public transportation, etc., and all those actions cannot be taken correctly if we don't consider the urban accessibility for all city users. Many studies revealed that incompatibility between the urban and architectural environment and the physical capacities of city user can lead to stress situation and dissuade to attend the city [2]. Urbanites and architects work together on challenging situations of stress in urban space and to design a city in line with the well-being of her users.

This multidisciplinary research invokes the human psycho-physiology dimension as a pertinent indicator of stress levels in urban space. Using knowledge ranging from urban studies [3] to information and communications technologies, this work aims to draw attention to original application of the sensor techniques in city studies.

Thus, to highlight those stress situations, we need to characterize them by analyzing the arousal levels via psychophysiological measures called EDA [4]. When an emotional arousal occurs, the brain receives signals translated by electrical changes at the skin surface.

Those psychophysiological signals are characterized by the succession of Skin Conductance Responses (SCR) [5] as illustrated in Figure 1, which represent the relationship between stress and EDA signal. Those skin conductance data represent events-related alertness, characterized through three components [6]:

-The amplitude: after stimulation, the signal resistance goes down to a minimum point; then it backs to its initial value. The amplitude of the SCR is measured by the difference between the maximum point and the minimum point of the signal.

- The duration d1: it is the time interval between the maximum point and the minimum point of the SCR

- The duration d2: it is the time interval between the point which marks the peak of the SCR and the point where the signal returns to 50% of the amplitude of the same reply.

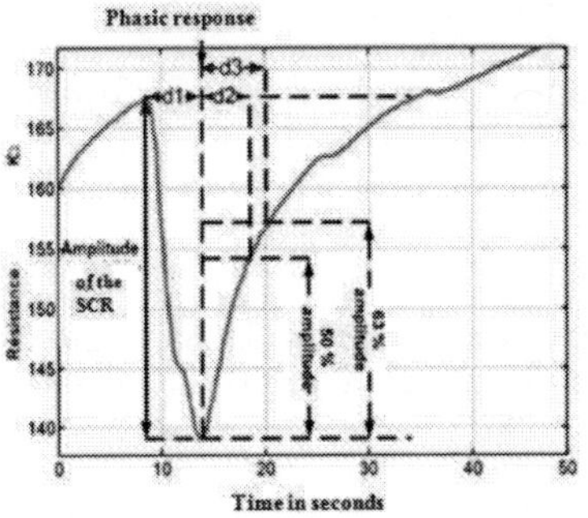

Figure 1. EDA variation and ocuurence of a SCR.

The SCR measures application covers a multitude of fields, such as health research, as well as urbanism discipline where they can be objective indicators of measuring arousal level when walking in the city [7]. Then, situations of stress can be identified and urban space accessibility and safety can be enhanced.

The remainder of the paper is organized as follows: Section 2 details the experimental protocol and the data collection process. Section 3 presents the results of an EDA and sound sources correlation. We discuss in Section 4 the relationship between stress situations and urban configurations. Section 5 concludes with a summary and an outline for few perspectives to this study.

II. EXPERIMENTAL PROTOCOL

This study is based on a multidisciplinary experimental protocol of three components:

- Spatial analysis: it's an urban graphic survey that shows urban crossroads (plans, spatial configurations, etc.) [8].
- Analysis of the physical signal: This part is divided into three parts: sound level measurements (acoustic metrology), audio records and analysis of spectral compositions.
- The perception of sound phenomena which is composed of two phases:
  - First, the commented walk method [9], which requests from the participant three simultaneous activities: walking, perceiving and describing what she/he heard. The aim of these walks was to obtain a full record of the multi sensorial perception in movement and the audio perception in particular. During each walk, we paid particular attention to behavioral indicators to help us analyze the relation between each subject and their surroundings [10][14].
  - Secondly, the capture of user's arousal (emotion) which is based on the capture of the physiological data during the commented walks by the biosensor (Q-Sensor). Emotional arousal is a form of EDA that increases during states of stress, anxiety or excitement and decreases during states of boredom, relaxation or indifference. Additionally, the sensor measured the participants' temperature and speed but also tracked their stress level [11][12].

A. *Material*

To realize this experimental protocol, we used these following devices:

- Q-sensor, which is a hand wear device; this is a biosensor of EDA (sampling frequency 32 Hz). It measures via the skin conductance the arousals, the temperature and the acceleration of the user for a 24-hour. Those data can be visualized thanks to software called "Q" (developed by the startup Affectiva from the Affective Computing Group of MIT Media Lab) [13]. It produces curves representing the EDA activity. Awareness' moments are detected through specific peaks.

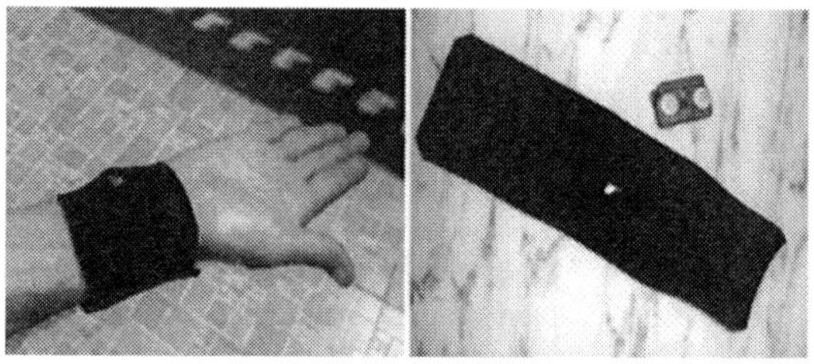

(A) (B)

Figure 2. The Q-Sensor.

- A digital voice recorder (sampling frequency 44,1 KHz). It is used to record the different sound sources along the walk. The dynamic frequency (spectrum) can be read by software called "audacity"
- A sonometer: A sound level meter that measures the noise levels. The unit used is the decibel, dB (A).

B. *Field of the study*

Our choice was fixed on the downtown of Tunis. This field is considered as a part of city development and urban growth articulation point between the south and the north of the capital. Our study focuses on two paths.

The first one, represented in red in the Figure 1, begins by the intersection between the *Yugoslavie* street and *Greece* street, then passes near the subway station « *Place Barcelone* » and ends at the intersection of the united Nations avenue, *Yougoslavie* street and *Farés El Khoury* street.

The second path is represented in green in Figure 1. It is located on the main avenue of the down town of Tunis, *Habib BOURGIBA*. Then, it passes by the most important crossroad "14 January square".

These walks include a variety of urban situations: a subway crossing, several potential crossroads, official establishments, bars and pedestrian walks. It is also known the trade activities on the ground floors and habitat and offices on the other floors building with three to ten floors).

It is divided into different sectors (zones), fig, according to variety of functions: in the first one, we note the diversity of the activities (mall, coffee shops, passage of the subway, etc.); the second zone is a habitation zone and small trades; then, the third one is a mechanic works' sector with buildings of just a ground floor or high ground floor; with the abundance of pedestrian walks. Finally, the forth sector is known by the importance of the traffic along the day and the rarity of the pedestrian walks and the trade markets. This diversity affects the quality of the soundscape.

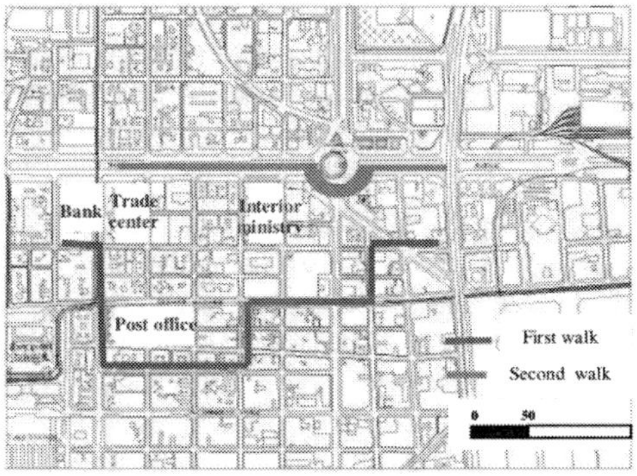

Figure 3. The field of the study.

C. *Population*

Our target population was about thirteen persons. In this paper, we will present the results of four cases: two men and two women, aged between 20 and 80 years. The experiments were made between 2010 and 2011. Each subject performed a commented walk in the itineraries previously chosen. Participants must wear the sensor just five minutes before the beginning of each walk (a necessary time for the sensor adaptation) [16]. During the experiment, we asked the subject to describe his feelings toward the ambiance and specially the sonic ambience. Here, the investigator's intervention should be minimal (just to remind the set point to the respondent) in order to not influence the participant.

III. RESULTS

To identify the different stress sound situation [15][17] [18], we have to correlate the different levels: the audio analysis, the physiologic data and the speech of the respondent.

In this section, we will present the EDA data collected from the two experiences (two walks).

A. *The first experience*

For the first experience, illustrated by Figure 4 and Figure 5, we will present the EDA curves of a man of 39 years old and a woman of 45 years old in the first path (represented in red in Figure 3). We obtain:

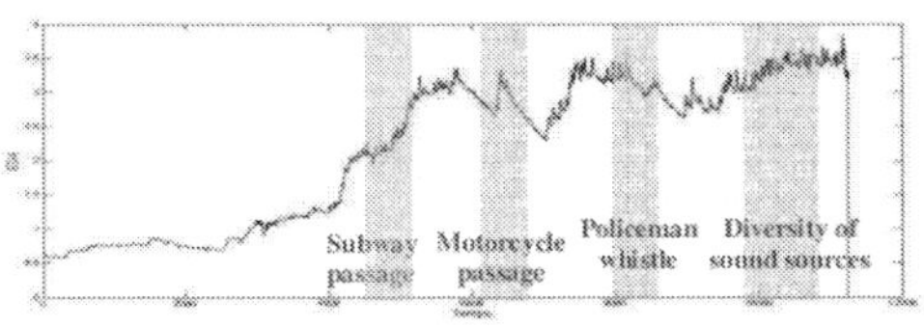

Figure 4. First experience: The EDA curve of the first subject.

We identify, in Figure 4, different sound stress situations (as explained in Figure 1). Some are related to particular sound sources (policeman whistle, passage of a motorcycle or the subway). We found that on the comments of the respondent *"The subway arrives. (...) And it bothers me"* or *"(...) I don't like **motorcycles** that speed after the turn"or "oh! The policeman whistle's is very disturbing!"* In other situations, we note also the multiplicity of the sound sources. *"The **noise becomes more important** than the other street. Especially here with this intersection, there is every kind of noise. I don't feel good anymore."*

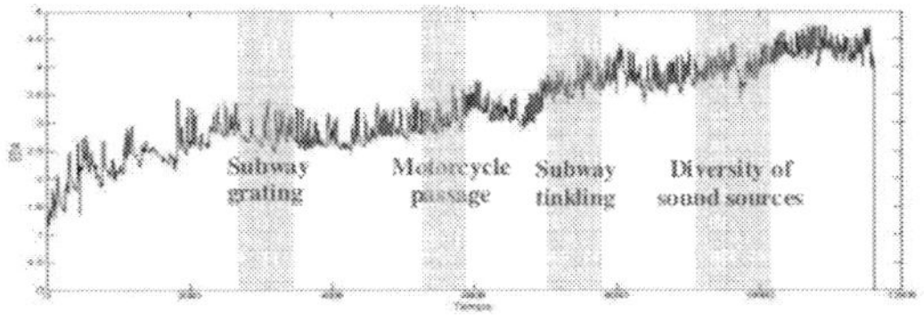

Figure 5. First experience: The EDA curve of the second subject.

In Figure 5, we note also two types of sound stress situations: due to particular sound sources and due to the diversity of the sources. This was confirmed by the comments of the users. "My *god! What's this sound? Oh! It's the subway grating*" and also *"But here it starts to fuss. (...) The noise increases, we approach the source of the noise, oh there are many here: Cars, pedestrians, motorcycles, hawkers...so, necessarily the tension rises*"

B. *The second experience*

For this experience, we will present, in Figure 6 and Figure 7 two EDA curves corresponding to two cases of a man of 83 years old and a woman of 63 years old in the second path (represented in green on Figure 3).

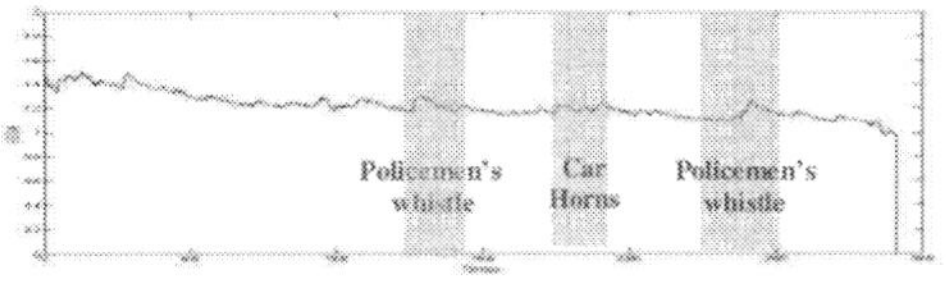

Figure 6. Second experience: The EDA curve of the first subject.

The sound stress situations detected in Figure 6 are linked mainly to the policeman whistle and the car horns even if the subject does not express clearly that she heard them. Due to age, elderly suffer from hearing loss and they cannot identify some sounds. This was confirmed by the EAD where we identified stressfull sound events but the participant expressed them in her comments leaning on the visual parameter: *"I hate this place, I can't deal with the cars...they don't respect pedestrian...Look! He is speeding with his car (...) There is a policeman, good job! I don't come here very often since I'm afraid from the traffic jam, I have difficulties to hear, and it's dangerous for me to go out of my home...*"

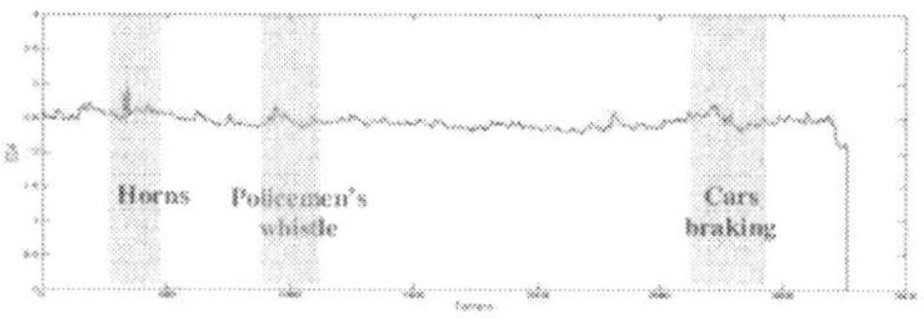

Figure 7. Second experience: The EDA curve of the second subject.

In Figure 7, we find the same disturbing sound sources, which are mainly the policeman whistle and the car brakes. The EDA of this subject reflect his stressful state by the succession of the SCR and the disturbed curve. This subject identified clearly the whistle's sound and after examining his clinical case, we discovered that he's wearing an internal audio prosthesis. These findings are confirmed by the verbal data: *"it's a crowded place! ...I don't feel secure, many cars and I can't even distinguish the traffic light to cross the road...Oh, and I'm listening to a whistle!!! A policeman, yes it's good (...) I hope he'll help me to cross, I'm feared...I have a headache".*

IV. Discussion

We will try in this section to correlate the results above by the audio data; so, we present in this paper just one case. We confront the EDA signal with the spectrum of audio signal recorded among the walk.

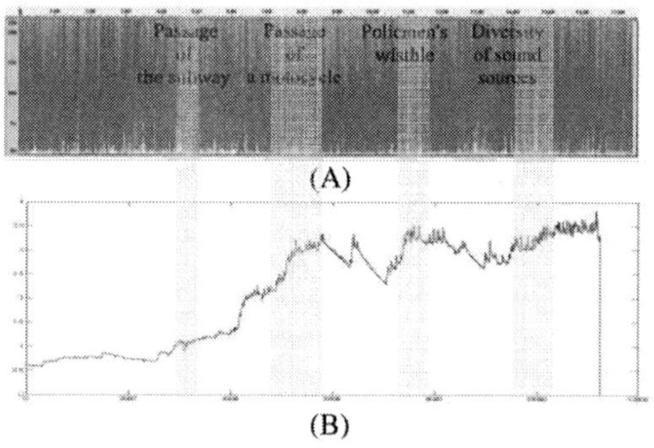

Figure 8. Correlation between the spectrum of the audio signal(A) and the EDA curve (B), case1.

The analysis of spectrum frequent of the audio signal highlights the physical characteristics of the urban space. Our setting is composed by a diversity of sound sources which compose an urban background sound made of high frequency of 10 kHz. We have note, also, in the last section that the stress feeling in the urban space, for the four cases presented in this paper, is linked to particular sound sources, situated on high and medium frequencies, such as the whistle of the policeman with 4 kHz, horns of the cars, grating and tinkling of the subway composed by signals between 8 kHz and 12 kHz and also, acceleration and braking of vehicles (cars, buses, motorcycles, etc.), which are high frequency signals by 12kHz.

By characterizing the complexity of the urban soundscape, we can conclude that the nature of the sounds and their frequency content are one of the causes of stress and discomfort feelings and emotions of the urban space users.

However, those results can be more discussed if we analyze with more accuracy EDA curves. In fact, the link between audio signal, EDA data and the commented walks cannot be highlighted if we don't consider the specificity of the urban configuration, the scene of the experience [19].

V. Conclusion

We presented in this paper an original approach of detecting arousal states via biosensors in city studies. In fact, according to the interest given to the question of pedestrian well-being and safety and how they experience the city, we developed a strategy to identify stress situations in urban space.

Through this multidisciplinary research, we adopted an exploratory approach to characterize the sound signal in order to detect the stressful information contained in complex soundscapes. By combining tools that qualify and quantify the informational content of the sound scene in the city, we achieved our task taking into consideration not only the audio parameter, but all senses, as a part of the multisensory experience of pedestrians in the city.

We were able to rich our goal thanks to the collaboration between many disciplines: architecture, psychophysiology, signal processing, urban design, etc. We identified stress situation by linking the sound event, the human perception and the urban configuration. It is important for architect to identify disabled spaces in the city that may cause problems for pedestrian, especially ones with disabilities, in order to correct them and to propose new urban design that may help to make the city safe for all users [20].

Among the perspectives of this work, we tend, using this protocol, to improve the graphical stage of any project realization with sound mappings for specific city users thereby improving the chances of their safety level during walking or crossing roads for equal accessibility of urban spaces by all users.

The affective dimension of the study represents a new response that shows potential on the perceptual dimension of a given category of city users [21]. The aptitude to personalize a given soundscape design while considering age, gender, physical and mental capacities of a specified class of population is an important step forward in a society that aspires for stress control. In that regard, a personalized study would be more useful instead of a group one. Such objective would be line with a global well-being.

ACKNOWLEDGMENT

We are particularly grateful to Professor Jean-Pierre PENEAU for framing this work. Our sincere gratefulness goes U2S team from the National School of Engineering of Tunis for helping on examining the analysis of frequency data and making algorithms of signal processing in particular misses Yosra Mzah, Asma Ameur and Olfa Fraj. We need to thanks also all participants of the experimental protocol for their collaboration and patience.

REFERENCES

[1] G. Moser, Les stress urbains, Paris, Armand Colin, 1992.

[2] P. Amphoux, G. Chelkoff, and J. P. Thibaud, Ambiances en débats, Grenoble: A la Croisée, p. 164, 2004.

[3] L. Saby, Vers une amélioration de l'accessibilité urbaine pour les sourds et les malentendants: quelles situations de handicap résoudre et sur quelles spécificités perceptives s'appuyer ? Thèse en génie civil. Institut National des Sciences Appliquées de Lyon. 358 p, 2007.

[4] R. W. Picard, "Emotion Research, by the People, for the People", Emotion Review 2 (3): 2010, pp. 250-254.

[5] W. Boucsein, Electrodermal Activity, University of Wuppertal, Wuppertal, Germany, second edition, 2012.

[6] R. Nocua, Conception et développement d'un système ambulatoire pour la mesure de l'activité du Système Nerveux Autonome pour la surveillance de personnes âgées à domicile, thèse de doctorat, Techniques de l'Ingénierie Médicale et de la Complexité, Université Joseph-Fourier, Grenoble, 176 p, 2009.

[7] B. Massot, Conception, réalisation de capteurs non-invasifs ambulatoires et d'exocapteurs embarqués pour l'étude et le suivi de la réactivité émotionnelle, PhD diss., University of Lyon, 2011.

[8] L. Ammar and Ph. Panerai, Tunis d'une ville à une autre Cartographie et histoire urbaine 1860-1935, Tunis : Espace Diwan, 2010.

[9] J. P. Thibaud, La méthode des parcours commentés, comment observer une ambiance ? Les cahiers de la Recherche Architectural. n°42/43, pp. 77-89, 1998.

[10] F. Hussein, Construction et expérimentation d'un protocole pour le traitement des ambiances sonores urbaines adapté aux personnes âgées presbyacousiques. Thèse en architecture. Spécialité ambainces architecturales et urbaines. Nantes, 330 p, 2012.

[11] R. Adhami, et al., ''Stress monitoring using a distributedwireless intelligent sensor system'', IEEE, Engineering in Medecine and Biology Magazine, 22(3), 2003, pp. 49-55.

[12] M. Z. Poh, N. C. Swenson, and R. W. Picard, "Wearable sensor for unobtrusive, long-term assessment of electrodermal activity", IEEE Trans Biomed Eng., 57(5): Feb. 2010, pp. 4352.

[13] R. Picard, "Future affective technology for autism and emotion communication, Philosophy Transactions of the Royal Society, Biological Sciences", vol. 364, no. 1535, pp. 3575-3584, 12 December 2009.

[14] F. Hussein, R. Ghozi, M. Jaïdane, and J. P. Péneau, ''Detecting hazardous situations faced by presbycusic pedestrians in cities: an audio-texture approach'', Ambiances [En ligne], Environnement - Modélisation- Caractérisation, March/April 2016. URL : http://ambiances.revues.org/485

[15] J. M. Auberlet, R. Bremond, and A. Tom, ''Pedestrians crossing: a psychological approach: Implications for pedestrian simulation'', Recherche Transports Sécurité 101, 2008, pp. 265–279.

[16] H. Bahri, R. Ghozi, F. Hussein, and D. Mallouch, ''Identification et caractérisation des états de stress par une segmentation probabiliste des signaux de l'activité électrodermale'', submitted to the 46th Journées des Statistiques, Rennes, France, 2014.

[17] R. Ghozi, O. Fraj, N. Khalfa, F. Hussein, and M. Jaidane, ''Presbyacusis and Stress Evaluation in Urban Settings'', 4th International Symposium on Applied Sciences in Biomedical and Communication Technologies, Barcelona, 2011.

[18]J. A. Healey and R. W. Picard, ''Detecting Stress During Real-World Driving Tasks Using Physiological Sensors'', IEEE Trans. On Intelligent Transportation Systems, 2005, pp. 156-166.

[19]L. Brown, ''Review of Progress in Soundscapes and an Approach to Soundscape Planning'', International Journal of Acoustics and Vibration, vol. 17, no. 2, 2012, pp. 7381.

[20] J. P. Péneau, ''L'approche ambiantale : une complexité augmentée'', SCAN'12, Paris, September 2012.

[21] J. P. Massabuau, Eloge de l'inconfort, Marseille, EditionsParenthèses, 2004.

Active Plasmonic Biosensors

Active plasmonic nanostructures in organic electroluminescent biosensors

Nan-Fu Chiu
Institute of Electron-optical Science and Technology
National Taiwan Normal University
Taipei, Taiwan
e-mail: nfchiu@ntnu.edu.tw

Yu-Chieh Yen
Institute of Electron-optical Science and Technology
National Taiwan Normal University
Taipei, Taiwan
e-mail: samuelyen0104@gmail.com

***Abstract*—We have demonstrated the phenomenon of active plasmonic grating structure for active surface plasmon polaritons propagating along 2-D grating at an organic/metal interface via Surface Plasmon Grating Coupled Emission (SPGCE) for enhancing and tuning far-field light emission. Our results showed that strong coupling resonances in SP-coupled emission from the interactions of organic/metal and metal/air symmetric mode lead to the enhanced optical properties of directional emission. Such scattering taking place through a metal film has an important bearing on the generation of useful light. Further investigations will be performed on SPPs with the integration of optimized organic electroluminescent plasmonic for active biosensor devices in biochemical analysis and immunoassay.**

Keywords- Surface plasmon resonance; nano-grating; band-gap; bioplasmonics.

I. INTRODUCTION

Surface Plasmon Resonance (SPR) phenomenon was described in 1980 and has been used for sensing for the past three decades [1][2]. SPR biosensors are optical sensors using polarized Surface Electromagnetic Waves (SEW) to probe molecular interactions between metal film surface and dielectric medium. SPR sensors have the advantages of high sensitivity, label-free and real-time detection [3]. In this paper, the coupling Surface Plasmon Polaritons (SPPs) on the nano-grating, the active plasmonics band-gap structure for bio-plasmonics are demonstrated. The presented results show that the enhanced performance of plasmonic on nano-grating, the active plasmonics band-gap structure is important for the structure design of novel optical biosensors.

The motivation of this research is to develop an accurate, integrated SPR sensor system chip using existing organic electroluminescent plasmonic technology due to its sensitivity and label-free advantage. We will propose a novel design of SPR device without using external light source and polarizer to have the same features of SPR, i.e., high sensitivity and real time. We can then observe the signal changes due to the presence of surface molecule or specific absorption wavelength of multiple samples. An all-in-one SPR sensor system chip with the capability of sensing applications in drug discovery, drug development testing or different kind of viruses and poison will be realized to eliminate large casualties in wars, terrorist activities or virus infections.

II. EXPERIMENT PROCEDURES

The excitation of organic semiconductor molecules by Surface Plasmon Grating Coupled Emission (SPGCE) is intended to demonstrate the effect of coupled active SPPs on the plasmonics response of a grating nanostructure with organic material on the surface. Our fabricated different pitch grating device consists of coupled organic/metal nanostructure with specific width and symmetric and asymmetric dielectric plasmonic band-gap structure. In particular, it is found that emission is significantly inhibited in the vicinity of the gap, and that the modified emission spectrum is determined by the wavelength dependence of the density of SPP states. We present recent experimental results discuss potential applications of such active plasmonic biosensor with enhanced resonance energy emission due to interactions on the organic/metal nano-grating. We report the design and development of organic semiconductor devices for chemical and biological sensing. A plasmonics-based biosensor was demonstrated using an organic SPGCE as an excitation source. In addition, the possibility of biological immunoassay for sensors based on active SPGCE was explored, as shown in Figures 1(a-c).

The interaction of SPR on a periodic grating of metal and polymer were investigated in theory and experiments [4]-[14]. In addition, we proposed a novel design of plasmonic biosensor without using the conventional external light source and polarizer to produce SPR having the same features, i.e., high sensitivity and real time. It can induce SPR wave on the metallic surface when proper resonant condition is matched by nano-grating coupled emission [4]-[7].

III. RESULTS AND DISCUSSION

We have shown experimentally that strong coupling between electronic and photonic resonances in metal grating and polymer grating really exist. Resonance angle plots of reflectivity of a metal nano-grating sensor, demonstrates the sensitivity of a refractmetric experiment, $\Delta\theta/\Delta n$=36.4 (λ=643 nm) and $\Delta\theta/\Delta n$=69.7 (λ=833 nm). In active plasmonic, our fabricated grating device of various pitches consists of coupled Au (gold) and polymer nanostructure with specific width and symmetric/asymmetric dielectric SP band-gap structure. In pitch modulation, results showed that grating at different pitch can match a linear shifting of momentum of about $\Delta k = 4.79\ \mu m^{-1}$ and $\Delta\theta = 11$ degree per 100 nm pitch size. In layer modulation, the resultant emission intensity can achieve a maximum enhancement of 6 times for the 4-Layer device and the Full-Width Half-Maximum (FWHM) was less than 50 nm. We can then observe the emission signal changes due to the presence of surface molecule or specific absorption wavelength of multiple samples. This phenomenon gives rise to a selective spectral response and a local field enhancement, which can be used for modulation in the nano-optics. The Alq_3/Au interface reciprocal interactions that the optical absorption, emission and scattering properties of metal nanostructures can be used to control the decay rates, intensity and FWHM and direction of luminescence emission.

The preliminary results of these prototypical systems based on active plasmonics look very promising. The use of active plasmonics may lead to new biosensors that are small, portable, inexpensive, fast, without the need of label-free or any chemical modifications, and biosensors that are capable of detecting low concentrations of specific analytes with high sensitivity, as well as selectivity, as shown in Figure 2 (a-c). We will optimize the active plasmonics and sensing component, which will have the benefit of expanding its application in various fields, including biochemical and antibody/antigen analyses, as well as enhancing its dynamic range due to the higher sensitivity. Such scattering taking place through a metal film has an important bearing on the generation of useful light. Further investigations will be performed on SPPs with the integration of optimized organic electroluminescent plasmonic for active biosensor devices in biochemical analysis and immunoassay. In our calculation, the grating pitch is set at 400 nm. Here, ε_d of air is 1, alcohol (1%) is 1.329, DNA (0.1mM) is 1.405, and Ethanol (1%) is 1.363 in our calculation. Figure 3 shows the calculation results from the SPR parameters given above. With an increasing value of ε_d, one can see a right shift of the ω-k curves, which correspond to an increase in momentum space.

IV. Conclusion

We demonstrated the SPGCE from excited organic layer on different metal grating in organic/metal structure. Our results showed that strong coupling resonances in SP-coupled emission from the interactions of Alq3/Au and Au/air symmetric mode leads to the enhanced optical properties of directional emission, intensity and FWHM for active plasmon devices. Such scattering taking place through a metal film has an important bearing on the generation of useful light. Further investigations will be performed on SPPs with the integration of optimized organic electroluminescent plasmonic for active biosensor devices in biochemical analysis and immunoassay. This indicated a potential application of disposable and point-of-care biosensor.

Acknowledgment

The authors would like to thank the Ministry of Science and Technology of the Republic of China, Taiwan, for financially supporting this research under Contract No. MOST 104-2221-E-003-023, MOST 103-2221-E-003-008, NSC 102-2221-E-003-021, and NSC 99-2218-E-003-002-MY3.

References

[1] A. Otto, Z. Phys. 216, 398-410 (1968).

[2] E. Kretschmann, Z. Phys. 241, 313-324 (1971).

[3] J. Homola, Surface Plasmon Resonance Based Sensors, Springer Series on Chemical Sensors and Biosensors (Springer-Verlag, Berlin-Heidelberg-New York, 2006).

[4] N.-F. Chiu, C.-D. Yang, Y.-L. Kao, and K.-L. Lu, Optics Express, 23 (8), 9602-9611 (2015).

[5] N.-F. Chiu, Teng-Yi Huang, Chun-Chuan Kuo, Chii-Wann Lin, and Jiun-Haw Lee, Applied Optics 52(7), 1383-1388 (2013).

[6] N.-F. Chiu, J.-H. Lee, C.-H. Kuan, K.-C. Wu, C.-K. Lee, C.-W. Lin, Appl. Phys. Lett. 91, 083114 (2007).

[7] N.-F. Chiu, C. Yu, J.-H. Lee, C.-H. Kuan, K.-C. Wu, C.-K. Lee, C.-W. Lin, Optics Express. 15, 11608 (2007).

[8] H. A. Atwater and A. Polman, Nat. Mater. 9(3), 205–213 (2010).

[9] N.-F. Chiu, C.-H. Hou, C.-J. Cheng and F.-Y. Tsai, Int. J. of Photoenergy, 2013, 502576 (2013).

[10] N.-F. Chiu, C.-J. Cheng, T.-Y. Huang, Sensors. 13(7), 8340-8351 (2013).

[11] W. L. Barnes and S. Wedge, Proceedings of SPIE Vol. 5450 (2004)

[12] D. K. Gifford, D. G. Hall, Appl. Phys. Lett. 81, 4315-4317 (2002).

[13] G. Winter and W. L. Barnes, Appl. Phys. Lett. 88(5), 051109 (2006).

[14] J. Feng, T. Okamoto, J. Simonen, and S. Kawata, Appl. Phys. Lett. 90, 081106 (2007).

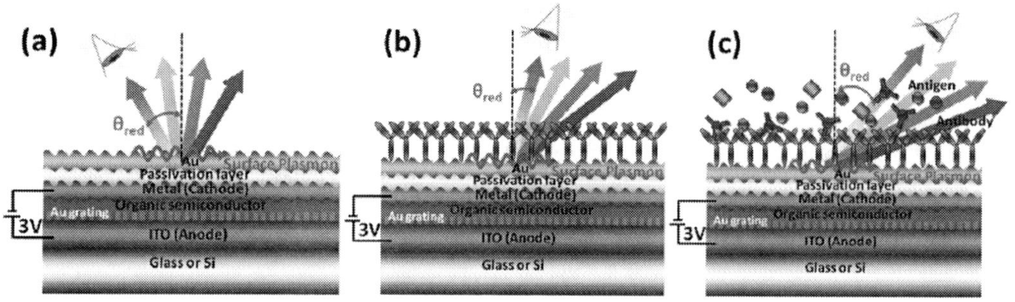

Figure 1. Light control in organic electroluminescence devices by SPGCE for biosensing application. The emission angle is dependent upon the index of refraction at the organic/metal/dielectric interface, which means that the index of refraction can be determined by measuring the shift in the emission angle.

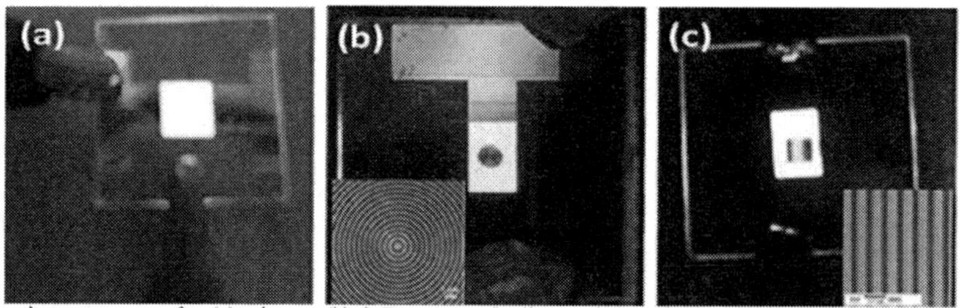

Figure 2. Active plasmonic grating structures for (a) planer, (b) 2-D concentrically grating and (c) 2-D rectangular lamellar grating in an organic/metal interface via surface plasmon coupled emission for enhancing and tuning far-field light emission of the active plasmonics biosensor based on novel electro-excitation method.

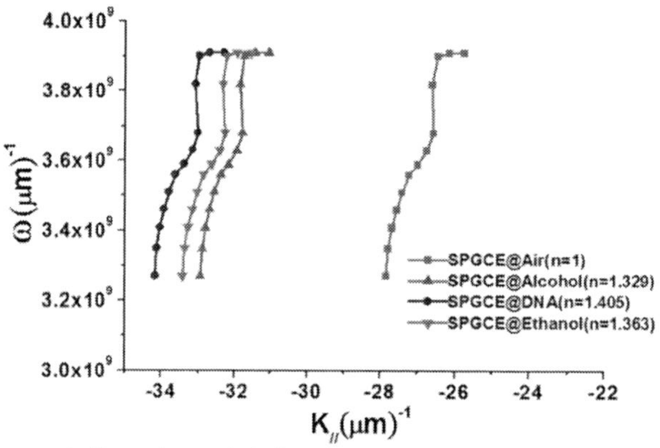

Figure 3.Experimental results for 2-D concentrically grating at pitch size of 400 nm. The dispersion relation between frequency ω and wave number $k_{//}$ for different species contacting the top side of the sample, the calibration dispersion curve for the determination of air and in alcohol (1%), DNA (0.1mM), and Ethanol (1%) solutions for the sample.

Impact Response of a Cantilever Beam Measured by Optical Fiber Sensors

Shiuh-Chuan Her[1] and Hsi-Wen Hou[2]
Department of Mechanical Engineering
Yuan Ze University
Tao Yuan, Taiwan
[1] e-mail:mesch@saturn.yzu.edu.tw
[2] e-mail:s945120@mail.yzu.edu.tw

***Abstract*—Mach-Zehnder interferometric technology combined with optical fiber sensor allows the direct measurement of the impact response of a cantilever beam. The difference in the optical path due to the strain induces a relative phase shift in the Mach-Zehnder interferometer. A 3 × 3 coupler is used to demodulate the phase shift of the Mach-Zehnder interferometer. Experimental results show that the optical fiber sensor is capable of measuring the dynamic strain of a cantilever beam impacted by a hammer. The impact responses measured by the optical fiber sensor are in good agreement with the strain gauge. The proposed optical fiber sensor is simple, inexpensive and easy to implement; moreover, it is highly reliable and accurate.**

Keywords- optical fiber sensor; Mach-Zehnder interferometer; dynamic strain; 3 × 3 coupler.

I. INTRODUCTION

Optical fiber sensors have attracted a great deal of attention in recent years due to their advantages over conventional sensors such as flexibility, embeddability, multiplexity, small size and immunity to electrical or magnetic interference. Optical fibers based on Fabry–P′erot interferometer (FFPI) have been utilized to measure electrical current [1] and the multiplexed interferometric current sensors have also been reported [2]. In this study, Mach-Zehnder optical fiber interferometric sensor is employed to measure the dynamic response of a cantilever beam subjected to impact. The method developed by Brown et al. [3] for demodulation of the phase shift is adopted. The demodulation scheme utilizes a 3 × 3 coupler to reconstruct the signal of interest. The experimental test results are validated with the strain gauge. In Section II, the Mach-Zehnder interferometer is briefly described. In Section III, the methodology of phase shift demodulation is discussed. In Section IV, the experimental test results for a cantilever beam are presented to demonstrate the feasibility of the proposed method.

II. MACH-ZEHNDER INTERFEROMETER

Mach-Zehnder interferometer consists of two 2 × 2 couplers at the input and output. The excitation is applied to the sensing fiber, resulting in an optical path difference between the reference and sensing fibers. The light intensity of the output of Mach-Zehnder interferometer can be expressed as [4]:

$$I = 2A^2(1+\cos\Delta\phi) \tag{1}$$

$$\Delta\phi = \frac{2\pi n_0}{\lambda}\left\{1-\frac{n_0}{2}\left[(1-\nu_f)p_{12}-\nu_f p_{11}\right]\right\}\int_{L_f}\varepsilon_f dx$$

where $\Delta\phi$ is the optical phase shift; n_0 is the refractive index of the optical fiber; λ is the optical wavelength, ν_f is the Poisson's ratio; p_{11} and p_{12} are the Pockel's constants; L_f and ε_f are the bonding length and strain of the optical fiber, respectively. Since the terms in front of the integral sign of (1) are constants for any given optical fiber system, the total optical phase shift $\Delta\phi$ is proportional to the integral of the optical fiber strain. By measuring the total optical phase shift, the integral of the optical fiber strain can be easily obtained as follows:

$$\int_{L_f}\varepsilon_f dx = \frac{\Delta\phi}{\frac{2\pi n_0}{\lambda}\left\{1-\frac{n_0}{2}\left[(1-\nu_f)p_{12}-\nu_f p_{11}\right]\right\}} \tag{2}$$

The integral of the strain in (2) denotes the change of the length of the sensing fiber which is surface bonded onto the host structure. The average strain of the optical fiber for optical phase shift $\Delta\phi$ is:

$$\varepsilon_{avg} = \frac{\int_{L_f}\varepsilon_f dx}{L_f} = \frac{\lambda\Delta\phi}{2L_f\pi n_0\left\{1-\frac{n_0}{2}\left[(1-\nu_f)p_{12}-\nu_f p_{11}\right]\right\}} \tag{3}$$

Thus, once the phase shift $\Delta\phi$ of the Mach-Zehnder interferometer is demodulated, the strain of the host structure can be determined by utilizing (3).

III. DEMODULATION OF PHASE SHIFT

To demodulate phase shift $\Delta\phi$ of the Mach-Zehnder interferometer, a 3 × 3 coupler is employed. It consists of a 1

× 2 coupler at the input and a 3 × 3 coupler at the output. The two outputs of the 1 × 2 coupler comprise the reference fiber and sensing fiber of the Mach-Zehnder interferometer. The sensing fiber is surface bonded onto the host structure. Mechanical or thermal loadings applied to the host structure, leads to an optical path difference between the two fibers. The difference in the optical path induces a relative phase shift in the Mach-Zehnder interferometer. The two optical signals are guided into two of the three inputs of a 3 × 3 coupler, where they interfere with one another. The methodology developed by Brown *et al.* [3] for demodulation of the phase shift is adopted.

IV. EXPERIMENTAL RESULTS

A cantilever beam impacted by a hammer is conducted in the experimental test. The beam of length L = 220 mm, width b = 20 mm, thickness h = 1 mm is made of copper with elastic modulus E = 120 GPa, density ρ = 8740 kg/m^3. An optical fiber is surface bonded to the middle of the cantilever beam as the sensing fiber of the Mach-Zehnder interferometer. The bonding length is L_f = 60 mm in this work. A schematic drawing showing the cantilever beam with optical fiber sensor is presented in Figure 1. The material properties for the optical fiber are: elastic modulus E_f = 72 GPa, Poisson's ratio ν_f = 0.17, index of refraction n_0 = 1.45, pockel's constants p_{11} = 0.12, p_{12} = 0.27, radius r_f = 62.5 μm. An electric resistance strain gauge is adhered to the cantilever beam near the optical fiber. The optical fiber sensing system is a Mach-Zehnder interferometer with a 3 × 3 coupler operating at the wavelength of λ = 1,547.28 nm. Figure 1 shows the signals of the three outputs of the 3 × 3 coupler. Substituting the three output signals of the 3 × 3 coupler as shown in Figure 2 into the Matlab software, performs the phase shift demodulation. The result of the demodulated phase shift is presented in Figure 3. Substituting the phase shift $\Delta\phi(t)$ from Figure 3 into (3), it leads to the determination of the dynamic strain of the cantilever beam. The dynamic strains obtained by the optical fiber sensor are compared with the results of the strain gauge as shown in Figure 4. Good agreement is achieved between these two sensors. The dynamic strain measured by the optical fiber sensor exhibits smooth and continuous oscillation, while a small perturbation and discontinuity appears at the peak of the oscillatory strain for the strain gauge. This demonstrates that the optical fiber sensor is more reliable and accurate compared with the strain gauge.

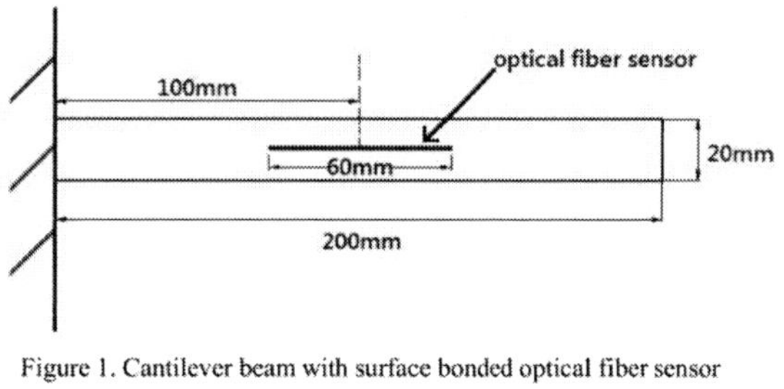

Figure 1. Cantilever beam with surface bonded optical fiber sensor

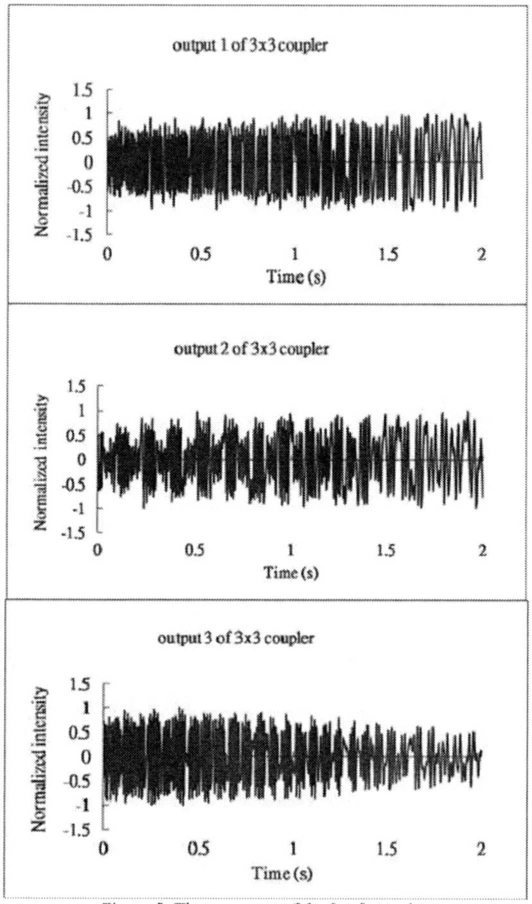

Figure 2. Three outputs of the 3 × 3 coupler

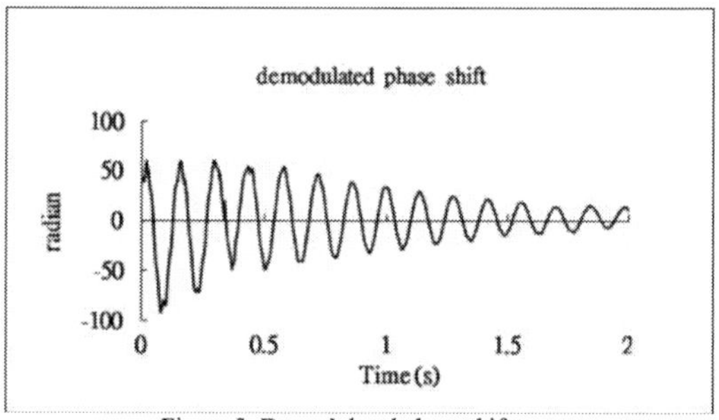

Figure 3. Demodulated phase shift

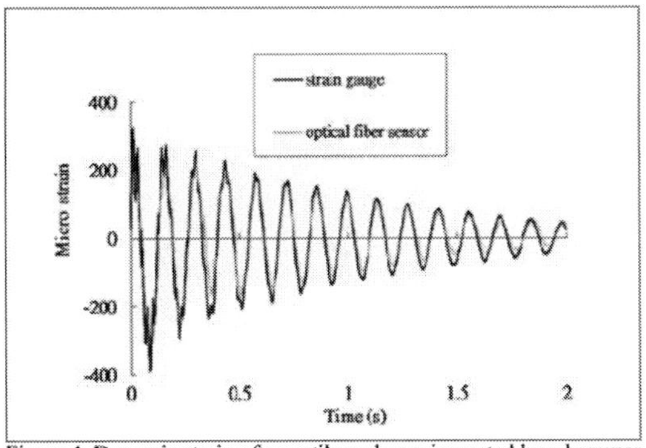

Figure 4. Dynamic strain of a cantilever beam impacted by a hammer

V. CONCLUSIONS

The dynamic strain of a cantilever beam subjected to impact by a hammer is determined using the optical fiber sensor. Mach-Zehnder interferometric technique is employed to measure the impact response. The impact responses measured by the optical fiber sensor are validated with the strain gauge. Good agreement is achieved between these two sensors. The proposed optical fiber sensor is simple, inexpensive and easy to implement. Moreover, its capability of measuring the impact responses with high reliable and accurate results demonstrates the novelty of present study.

REFERENCES

[1] Y. Park, W. Seo, C.E. Lee, and H.F. Taylor, "Fiber Fabry–P´erot type optical current sensor with frequency ramped signal processing scheme," J. Opt. Soc. Korea, vol. 2, 1998, pp. 74–79.

[2] H. Lin and S.C. Huang, "Fiber-optics multiplexed interferometric current sensors," Sens. Actuators A, vol. 121, 2005, pp. 333–338.

[3] D. A. Brown, C. B. Cameron, R. M. Keolian, D. L. Gardner, and S. L. Garrett, "A symmetric 3 × 3 coupler based demodulator for fiber optic interferometric sensors," Proc. SPIE, vol. 1584, 1991, pp. 328-335.

[4] J. S. Sirkis, "Unified approach to phase-strain-temperature models for smart structure interferometric optical fiber sensors: Part 1, development." Opt. Eng., vol. 32, 1993, pp.752-761.

Flexible Gas Sensors Fabricated by Ultrasonic Spray Deposition

Sandrine Bernardini [1], Marc Bendahan [1]
Aix – Marseille Université, IM2NP – UMR CNRS 7334,
Marseille, France
email: sandrine.bernardini@im2np.fr
email: marc.bendahan@im2np.fr

Monica Acuautla [2]
Zernike Institute for Advanced Materials
University of Groningen
Groningen, The Netherlands
email: m.i.acuautla.meneses@rug.nl

Emmanuelle Pietri [3]
Genes'Ink
Rousset, France
email: Emmanuelle.pietri@genesink.com

Abstract — **Sensors are changing the way people live and considerable efforts are under way for their integration into daily devices. Recently, much attention has been given to sensor fields for flexible and printed electronics. Among all the processes, ultrasonic spray deposition is a simple and precise technique giving enormous potential for applications with low cost production, low waste of material and thin film uniformity. In this work, we are focusing on Zinc Oxide nanoparticles deposited by ultrasonic spray on a flexible substrate as sensitive layer for air quality monitoring. The flexible platform consists of Ti/Pt interdigitated electrodes for gas detection and a micro-heater device, both on Kapton HN substrate. A brief description of the process steps will be provided. Gas sensing properties have been investigated and the flexible sensors present repeatable responses toward ammonia (NH_3) and ozone (O_3) with fast responses and recovery times in a wide range of gas concentrations. The optimum working temperatures were experimentally determined at 300 °C for NH_3 and 200 C° for O_3. Overall, this work highlights the ultrasonic spray potential for fast processing flexible gas sensors based on zinc oxide solution.**

Keywords-Flexible gas sensor; ultrasonic spray deposition; ozone sensor; ammonia sensor; kapton substrate; ZnO ink.

I. INTRODUCTION

The market for printed, flexible and organic electronics is growing exponentially with huge potential and new applications in our daily life. New sensors are emerging in various applications, and the fabrication techniques could be key to reach some benefits such as improved performance, flexibility, transparency, reliability, and better environmental credentials. Ultrasonic spray deposition is a good candidate to fabricate thin film at a lower cost in a large area with low material waste avoiding expensive chemical solutions and high temperatures, which are not suitable with flexible substrates [1][2]. Moreover, "ultrasonic technology nozzle-less" delivers a thinner and more precise coating application than conventional spray nozzles, film coaters, roll coaters, and jetting technology.

In this work, ZnO nanoparticle films were deposited by ultrasonic spray nozzle–less on DuPont™ Kapton HN polyimide substrate using ink solution from Genes'Ink company (reference ZnO5F12). The interdigitated electrodes and the micro–heater device were fabricated using photolithography [3]. In Section II, the sensor process will be described and the results will be discussed in Section III.

II. DESCRIPTION OF APPROACH AND TECHNIQUES

Our flexible gas sensor consists of a 75µm thin Kapton polyimide film, with Ti/Pt interdigitated electrodes for gas detection, and a Ti/Pt micro-heater device allowing an efficient control of temperature, useful for detection of gases. Kapton polyimide film presents the advantage of working up to 400 °C with an excellent thermal stability. Furthermore, it is solvent resistant and flexible. The metal electrodes Ti/Pt were deposited by magnetron sputtering with thicknesses of 5 nm and 100 nm, respectively. In this work, ZnO nanoparticles were used as sensitive material with a thickness of 100 nm deposited by ultrasonic spray. It is a simple technique ideal for the thin and uniform application of several materials with low viscosity. Furthermore, it ensures very little waste of coating material. The deposition was done with a programmable nozzle–less spray machine Prism BT Benchtop X-Y-Z Coating System from Ultrasonic Systems, Inc. (USI manufacturer) that gives thin film thickness homogeneity with an error around ± 4 % on A4 sheet of Kapton HN. The operational principle consists in the product being applied into a rectangular tip through a liquid applicator. The spraying takes place by the vibration of a titanium transducer and due to the rectangular tip, the coating pattern is rectilinear, flat and uniform [4]. The ZnO films obtained were annealed for 3 hours at 300°C to improve their quality and stability. The gas measurements were carried out in a closed chamber by measuring the resistance through the sensitive material at different temperatures from 25°C to 350°C under a target exposure of 1 minute in order to find the best operating conditions. We used a power supply to control the operating temperature and a source meter Keithley 6430 for the data acquisition.

III. RESULTS AND DISCUSSION

A. *Flexible gas sensors*

The gas sensor fabricated with ZnO nanoparticles as sensitive material and deposited by ultrasonic spray technique is presented in Figure 1.

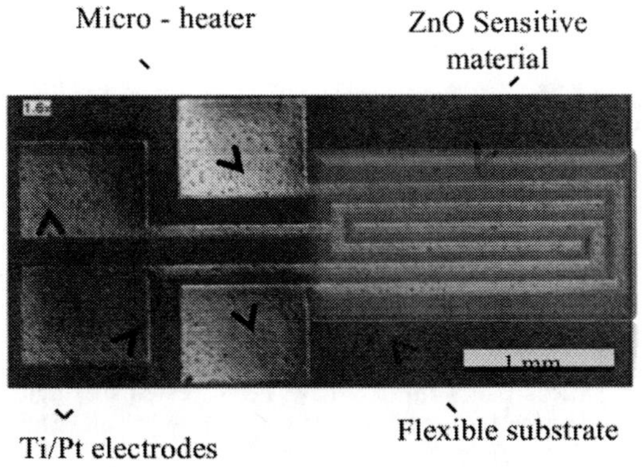

Figure 1. Sensor fabricated on flexible substrate.

B. *Response to Ammonia and Ozone*

Figure 2 shows good sample responses and a wide range of detection from 10 ppm to 100 ppm for ammonia. The best working temperature has been determined at 300°C.

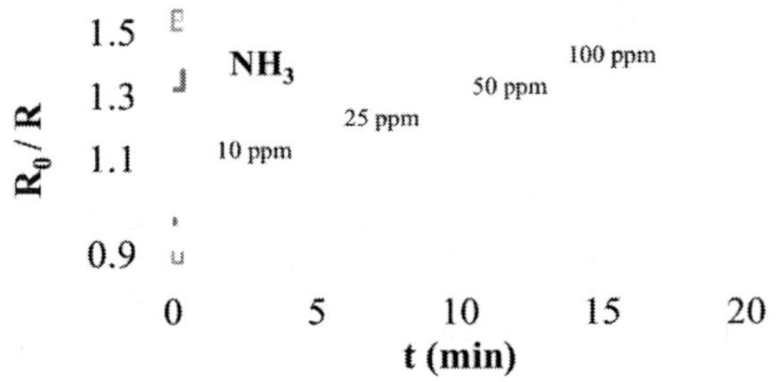

Figure 2. Sensor responses deposited by ultrasonic spray under NH_3 at 300 °C.

The response time is defined as the time taken by a sensor to achieve 90% of the total signal change when the sensor is exposed to a target gas [5][6][7]. Similarly, the recovery time is defined as the time it takes to reach 90% of the difference between the equilibrium resistance under target gas and the sensor resistance in dry air after the gas injection was stopped (i.e. in dry air with no gas) [8]. We observed good and fast responses, with recovery times of less than 2 minutes, and a good detection range for ammonia. Responses to ozone during the same exposure time have also been registered and the best working temperature has been found at 200°C. Figure 3 presents the response at 200°C under ozone from 5ppm to 300ppb. This exposure time did not allow reaching the response peak saturation as in the case of ammonia. However, for an exposure time of 1 minute the responses are always fast for all concentrations as well as the time to come back to the baseline.

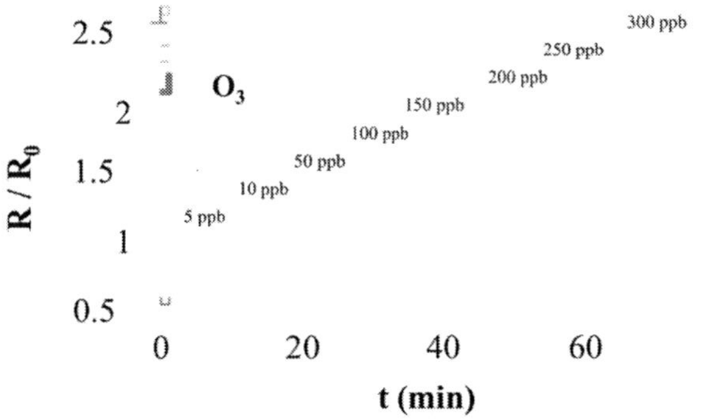

Figure 3. Sensor responses deposited by ultrasonic spray under O_3 at 200 °C.

This coating technique presents important benefits such as good thin film distribution and good control of the deposit parameters.

IV. CONCLUSION

The gas measurements in our experiments showed good responses with fast response / recovery times towards ammonia (at 300 °C) and ozone (at 200 °C) in a wide range of gas concentrations. The obtained gas sensing properties on Kapton HN substrate and the use of ultrasonic spray deposition highlight the promising opportunity in the flexible electronic field to fabricate quality devices with fast and low cost production.

ACKNOWLEDGMENT

The authors would like to acknowledge the research grant of CONACyT-MX (214895/310187), and A. Combes for his technical support in this work.

REFERENCES

[1] D. Perednis, "Thin film deposition by spray pyrolysis and the application in solid oxide fuel cells", PhD-Swiss Federal Institute of technology Zurich, 2003, pp. 1–165. Diss. Eth No. 15190.

[2] J. Narro-Rios, M. Ramachandran, and D. Martínez-Escobar, "Ultrasonic spray pyrolysis deposition of SnSe and $SnSe_2$ using a single spray solution", Journal of Semiconductors, 34, 2013, pp. 013001-1–013001-4.

[3] M. Acuautla, et al. "Ozone flexible sensor fabricated by photolithography

[4] and laser ablation process based on ZnO nanoparticles", Sensors and Actuators B, 203, 2014, pp. 602–611.

[5] Precision coating technology available on http://www.ultraspray.com (accessed on April 2016).

[6] Y. Abdi, S. M. Jebreiil, and P. Afzali, "Resonantly excited ZnO nanowires for fabrication of high sensitivity gas sensor", Current Applied Physics, 14, 2014, pp. 227–231.

[7] X. Yu, F. Song, B. Zhai, C. Zheng, and Y. Wang, "Electrospun ZnO nanotubes and its gas sensing applications", Physica E, 52, 2013, pp. 92–96.

[8] C. Wang, L. Yin, L. Zhang, D. Xiang, and R. Gao, "Metal oxide gas sensors: Sensitivity and influencing factors", Sensors, 10, 2010, pp. 2088–2106.

[9] D. K. Aswal and S. K. Gupta, "Science and technology of chemiresistor gas sensors", Nova Science publishers 2006.

A Comprehensive Investigation of the Electrical Features of Commercial Resistive Flex Sensors

Giovanni Saggio
Dept. Electronic Engineering
University of Rome "Tor Vergata"
Rome, Italy
saggio@uniroma2.it

***Abstract*— Resistive flex sensors have been gaining more and more importance in the latest years. They are applied in many and different fields ranging from human body tracking, traffic safety, musical instruments and so on. These sensors have the mechanical advantage to be low-weight, unobtrusive and pliable. However from an electrical point of view different works have been devoted to investigate single properties, but there is a lack of a comprehensive investigation, useful to select the proper sensor for the proper application. This paper is devoted to fill this lack.**

Keywords-resistive flex sensor; bend sensor.

I. Introduction

A Resistive Flex Sensor (RFS hereafter) consists typically of a thin flexible substrate painted on-top with a polymer ink, which includes conductive particles moved apart when the sensor is bent away (outward) from the ink. Because of the distances of the particles, an outward bending produces an increasing of the RFS impedance, which was demonstrated to be substantially resistive (real), since the reactive (imaginary) part is practically negligible [1]. The change in resistance is fully reversible; so that the sensor returns to its initial value when straighten.

RFSs are furnished without or with a protective coating layer, useful for chemical/mechanical protection when necessary. In the first occurrence RFSs are known as uncoated (or base, or bare), otherwise as coated (or over-laminated). Regarding all the different technological material and procedures in developing RFSs, the interested reader can find a comprehensive review in [2].

RFSs having only one layer printed with the conductive ink do not usefully respond when bent in the opposite side (inward) from the ink. Only the two-layer engineered types can respond both increasing and decreasing their resistance with both outward and inward mechanical bending.

In the latest years, RFSs have been widely adopted for different purposes. Examples are bio-metrics (placement or movement of patients/athletes) [3], robotics (in realizing position feedback mechanism) [4], virtual-reality (user equipped with a sensory glove integrating RFSs virtually interact with objects on a PC screen) [5], automotive (for car occupant or traffic safety) [6] [7], musical instruments (transforming common gestures into sound creation) [8], assistive technologies (for communication of speechless users) [9], and so on.

Despite their widespread usage, as far as we know, only single electrical issues of RFS have been treated in single papers, and some features have not been treated at all. This paper is aimed to fill this lack.

In particular, our investigation of the electrical features of commercial RFSs considers the electrical resistance R versus angle of bending α (expressed as $R=R(\alpha)$), the overall electrical variation ΔR, the sensitivity $S=\Delta R/\Delta\alpha$, the repeatability, the hysteresis and the step response decay. In addition, all these aspects are here analyzed with respect to the RFS bending around pivots of different radiuses (0.6cm, 0.8cm, 1.0cm, 1.2cm), RFS differently over-laminated (none, polyester, polyamide), with different length (1", 2", 3", 4.5"), and with inward (-90° to 0°) and outward bending (0° to 120°).

In principle, RFSs can be indigenously prepared for custom design (an example explained in [10], but our investigation focuses on the mostly used RFSs, which are commercialized by Flexpoint (FP hereafter, www.flexpoint.com) and Spectrasymbol (SS hereafter, www.spectrasymbol.com), in particular the one-layer engineered types (also known as *unipolar*) being the most adopted ones.

Section II reports details about the RFSs we adopted and the designed set-up used to characterize them.

Section III is devoted to the outputs of the measurements and the resulting comments and suggestions useful for the selection of the right sensor for the right application.

Section IV concludes with some remarks.

II. Materials and Methods

RFSs by FP come in one uncoated version and in two coated versions (realized by means of polyester and polyamide respectively) and in three lengths of 1", 2" and 3" respectively (Figure 1a). As a peculiarity, the SS RFSs are born with an inner high resistance of their conductive ink (in the MOhm range), so that some metallic pads are added (Figure 1b) to lower this high-value resistance to more convenient values.

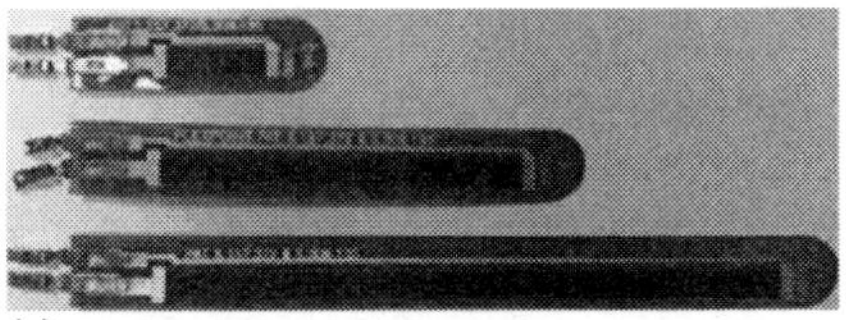

(a)

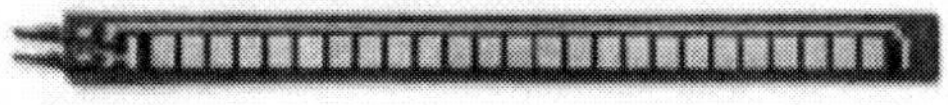

(b)

Figure 1. (a) FP RFSs with different length of 1", 2", 3" and (b) SS 4.5" lenght RFS with additional metal pads visible on-top (at bottom).

The SS manufacturer does not provide any information regarding an eventual coating layer.

Table 1 summarizes the different types of RFSs under tests. Differences are in manufacturer, over-lamination and length.

TABLE I. DIFFERENT TYPES OF RFSS USED FOR OUR TESTS

Flexpoint		
Code	***Overlamination***	***Lenght***
A15, B11, G6, H6, H15, I15, I17	none	2"
A17, C15, I12	polyamide	2"
B10, D11, F16	none	3"
C1, C14	polyester	3"
C5, H11, N7	none	1"
E3	polyamide	3"
G5, G14, J4	polyester	2"
SpectraSymbol		
S1, S2, S3, S4, S5, S6, S7	unknown	4.5"

The electrical features of the RFSs were obtained by means of a fully automatized set-up, so to overcome, as far as possible, human subjected errors. The core of the set-up was a mechanical hinge, with one leaf fixed on an anti-vibrating bench, and one leaf welded to a central cylindrical pin and rotating with it. The rotation was obtained by means of a stepper motor (PD-109-57 by Trinamic, Hamburg, Germany). Each RFS was laid along the hinge so to bend according to the rotation of the mobile leaf (Figure 2). Four different hinges were utilized, with different diameters of the pin, 0.6, 0.8, 1.0 and 1.2cm respectively.

Data were acquired by means of a multimeter (Agilent 34405, by Agilent, Santa Clara, CA, USA), and the overall system was controlled via LabVIEW routines (Laboratory Virtual Instrumentation Engineering Workbench, by National Instruments, Austin, TX, USA). The ad-hoc realized LabVIEW graphical interface consisted of different sections with commands devoted to set/acquire data from the motor and the multimeter (Figure 3).

Figure 2. The RFS lies on a hinge having one leaf rotated by means of a stepper motor (not visible in the figure)

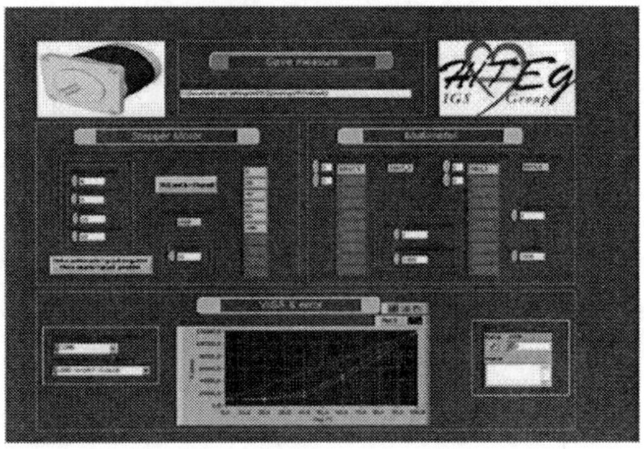

Figure 3. The graphical interface useful to control instruments and to acquire data from the sensors

All tests were performed in a room with fixed and controlled temperature (20°C) and humidity (40%).

Each RFS was tested bending it from 0° to -90° to 0° (inward "round trip" bending) and from 0° to 120° to 0° (outward "round trip" bending), each cycle ("trip") ten times iterated. The mobile leaf was rotated at 20 degree/sec, and paused every 5° to allow 10 data averaged acquisition during 500ms. For the "step response decay" test, each RFS was simply randomly flexed and then returned to the flat position maintained for 60min, during which data were continuously acquired.

III. RESULTS AND DISCUSSION

A. R vs. α

Let us start considering the RFS electrical behavior in terms of resistance R versus bending angle α, "R vs. α".

Figure 4(a) shows how sensors of the same type and length offer a different interval of resistance even when bent by the same amount, which seems to indicate the necessity to measure all RFSs, one-by-one, before their adoption. However, Figure 4(b) evidences a common trend for all the sensors with normalizing resistance data to 0-1 range. In particular, for simplification purposes, if we can accept roughly a 12% of maximum error, we can adopt a unique average curve for all the sensors, as evidenced in Figure 5.

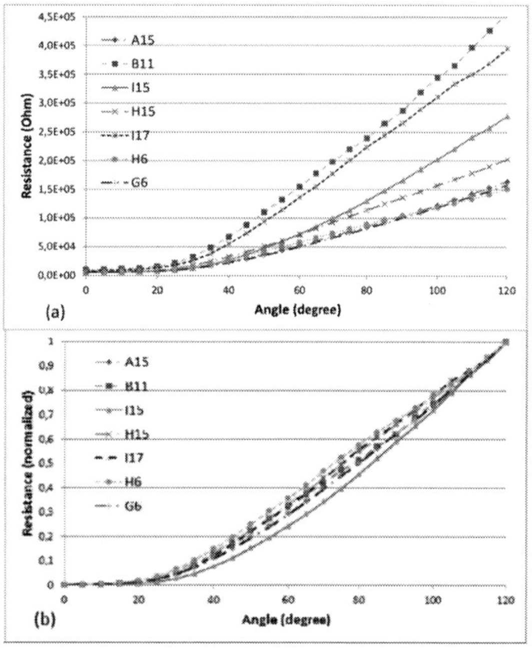

Figure 4. R vs. α (a) one-by-one and (b) normalized curve of uncoated FP RFSs

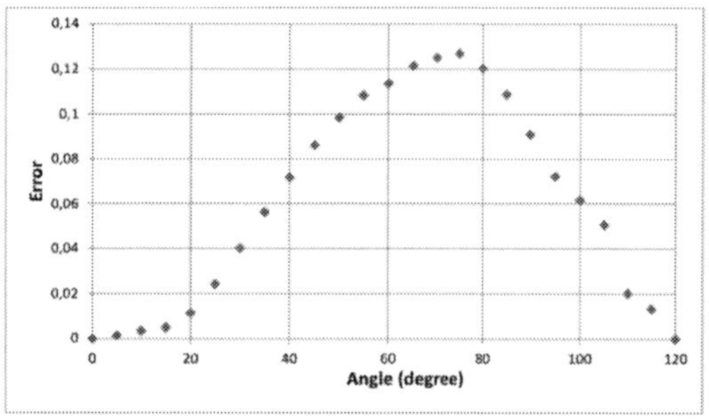

Figure 5. The maximum differences in resistance between normalized curves at each agle of bending for the ncoated FP RFSs

Similarly, the FP polyamide-coated and polyester-coated samples demonstrated different "R vs. α" curves (Figure 6a, b), but all with a similar trend, highlighted when a comparison is performed among the normalized versions of the curves.

We interpolated all the previous "R vs. α" curves using the "polyfit" function of Matlab (by MathWorks®, Inc.), that is a polynomial fitting, with the related fit error evaluated in terms of "residuals" (differences between the response data and the fit to the response data).

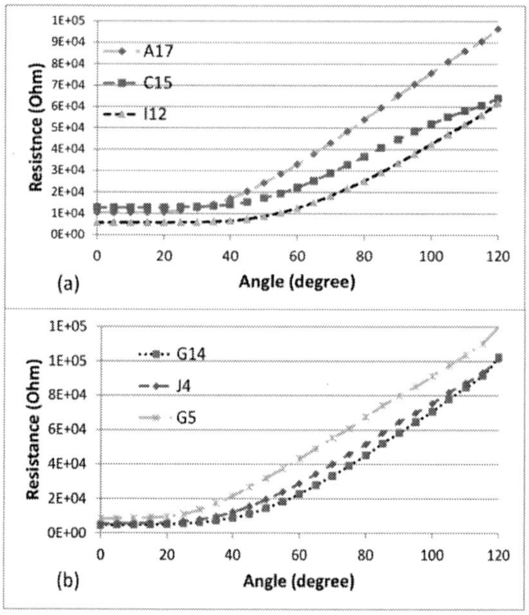

Figure 6. R vs. α curves for FP (a) polyamide and (b) polyester samples

Table II shows that a 6th degree polynomial curve fitting presents residuals as low as ~2.3%, ~2.5%, ~1.2% respectively for A15, J4, C15 samples, in comparison to a "simple" linear approximation. A polynomial higher than six degree does not produce meaningful advantages. Anyway, the 6th degree polynomial claims the sensor to be subjected to a time-expensive calibration procedure before its usage, since it is necessary to bend it at six different angles and acquiring the relative resistance values to obtain the six coefficients of the equation.

TABLE II. RESIDUALS WITH RESPECT TO THE EQUATION DEGREE

Equation degree	Residuals		
	A15	*J4*	*C15*
1st	54909	40757	28134
2nd	13240	10875	9129
3rd	4186	4367	5734
4th	3405	3863	2121
5th	2232	1220	1300
6th	1262	1014	345
7th	1127	983	310
8th	1115	882	275
9th	1012	871	176
10th	957	871	172

A convenient alternative can be to consider a step-wise linearization: a linear fitting within 0°-40° range and another linear fitting within 40°-120° range. In such a manner, the angle range versus R^2 couples "$\Delta\alpha$;R^2" are:

- sample A15: "0°-40°; 0.8275" and "40°-120°;0.9962"
- sample J4: "0°-40°;0.7878" and "40°-120°;0.9963"
- sample C15: "0°-40°; 0.7977" and "40-120°;0.9929"

Although these results are obtained for special cases (in particular for FP uncoated, polyester-coated and polyamide-coated 2" RFS samples), the same results can be usefully generalized for any FP RFSs, because of the possibility of normalization already discussed.

When the non-linearity can be a relevant issue, linearization procedures ca be adopted, such as to insert a standard fixed-value resistor in parallel to the RFS under test [11], or to cut the RFS in a shape different from the standard rectangular one [12] or, finally, to add a coating layer [11], but waiving to the advantage of the greater sensitivity and, in fact, turning to the coated occurrence.

Differently from the FP RFSs, the SS ones demonstrate an inner high degree of linearity (R^2=0.997), as shown in Figure 7.

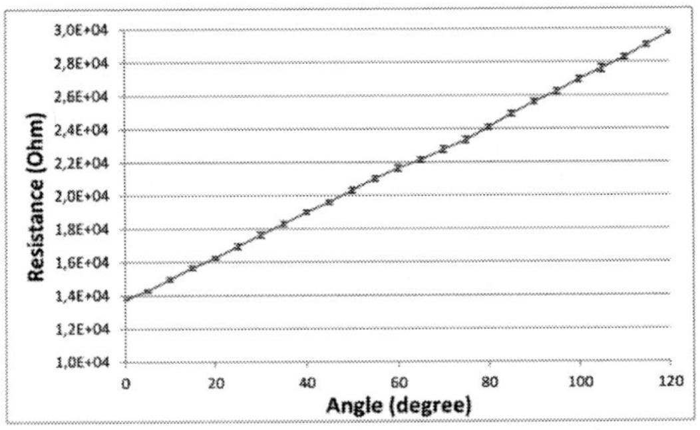

Figure 7. The SpecrtaSymbol RFSs demonstrate an inner high degree of linearity of the "*R* vs. *α*" curve.

In a previous work a mechanical model of the RFSs was developed to demonstrate that isotropy, of both the supporting layer and the on-top engineered sensible material, claims linearity of the "*R* vs. *α*" curve [13]. That demonstration suggests that FP RFSs are made of anisotropy elements and that SS RFSs have isotropy body. Another hypothesis for the linearity of the SS RFSs can result from the added metallic pads. In fact, as reported in [11], one method to linearize a non-linear behavior of an RFS is to add a parallel resistance and those pads can similarly "operate" as a sort a current-divider resistor.

B. Sensitivity

The FP polyamide-coated, polyester-coated and bare RFSs have higher sensitivity $S=\Delta R/\Delta\alpha$ for angles >40°, >25° and >18° respectively, as reported in Figure 8.

For lower angles the FP RFSs sensitivity is reduces and comparable to the one of the SS RFSs.

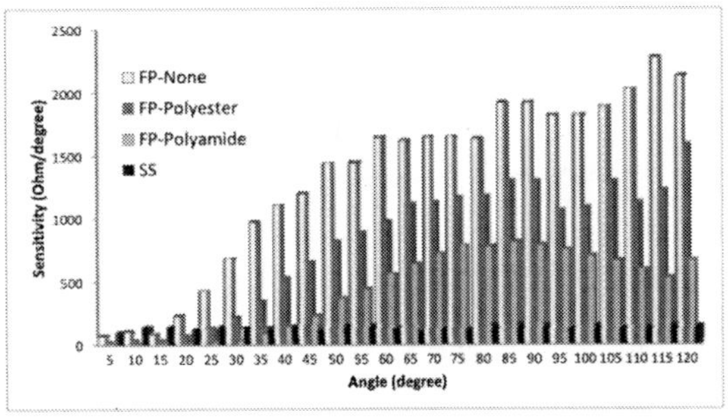

Figure 8. Sensitivity versus bending angle for all types of RFSs

C. Repeatability and hysteresys

Among the specific features of a RFS, it is important that such a sensor can perform without any meaningful variation in measurement when subjected to the same testing conditions, i.e. to offer repeatability. In addition, it is relevant to observe if the resistance value, acquired at the same angle, is maintained when tests are performed when the stepper motor both increases the angle value and lowers the angle values, i.e. if RFS performs without meaningful hysteresis.

All our tests were ten times iterated, and we evaluated the repeatability of the measures in terms of the standard deviation (SD) expressed in percentage. Figure 9 summarizes the obtained results.

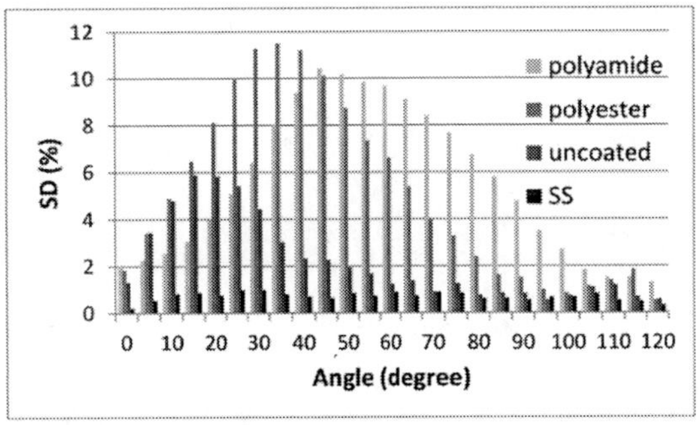

Figure 9. SD(%) versus bending angle for all types of RFSs

It can be evidenced that a lower, and practically constant SD(%) results for the SS RFSs at all the tested angles. The FP RFSs perform with higher SD(%) in particular for middle angles, and the coated versions perform with higher SD(%), therefore a lower repeatability.

Regarding the hysteresis, all RFSs performed with values lower than the respective SD, so that we can affirm that it is practically irrelevant.

D. R vs. pin radius

The resistance variation in bending a RFS is necessarily proportional to the portion of its length effectively flexed. Therefore, it is reasonable to experience higher resistance variation for lower value in diameter of the pin of the hinge. Figure 10 reports the resistance trend for the special case of the FP RFS B11 sample with different pins of 0.6, 0.8, 1.0 and 1.2cm in diameter. Although this is just an example, we experienced the same trend for all our FP RFSs samples.

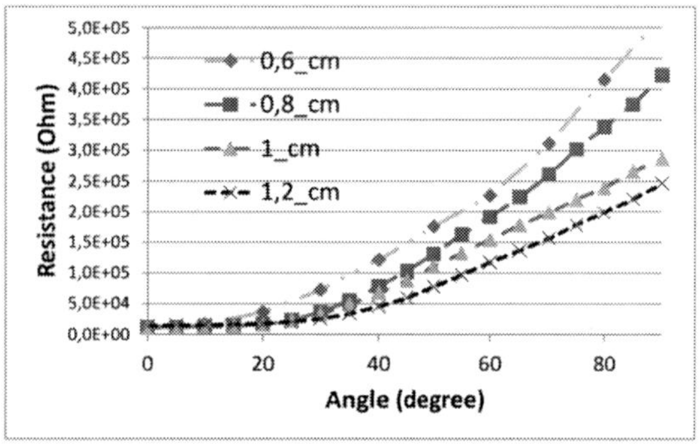

Figure 10. Comparison of resistance variation trends of the FP B11 sample when flexed around pins with different diameter

E. *Different coatings*

An additional layer, on-top of the conductive one, can help in mechanical protection and increase the possible cycle of bending mechanical stress before failures of the sensor. This is why some types of RFSs come with some coatings, in particular made of polyester or polyamide. However, the advantages resulted from a mechanical point of view affect the sensors electrical performances. In particular, our tests evidenced a reduction in the range (max-min) of resistance variation, more evident with the polyamide coating with respect the polyester one, as evidenced in Table III. Regarding the SS RFSs, those sensors resulted with the lower range, possibly due to the metallic pads, since there is no evidence of a coating.

TABLE III. COMPARISON OF MIN, MAX AND RANGE OF AVERAGE RESISTANCE VALUES OF DIFFERENT RFSS

RFS type	Resistance		
	min	*max*	*range*
FP uncoated	6839	257756	250917
FP polyester	6279	107904	101625
FP polyamide	9605	74124	64519
SpectraSymbol	13783	29750	15967

Again, also in spite of the coating layer, the FP RFSs result with the same trend in "*R* vs. α" curves, as evidenced in Figure 11 reporting the normalizing resistance data to 0-1 range.

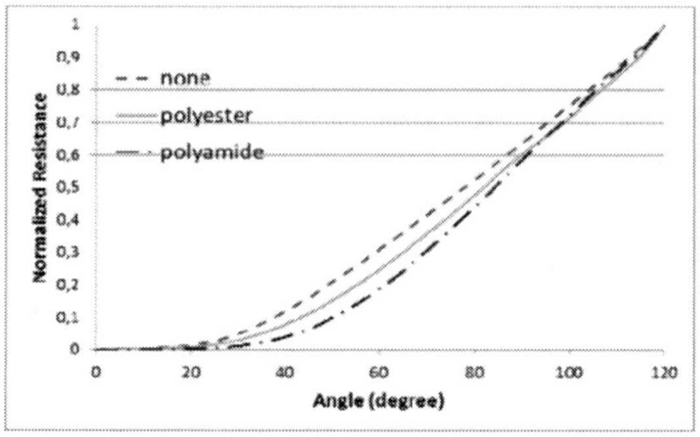

Figure 11. Normalized resistance versus bending angle for FP RFSs differently over-laminated.

F. *Inward bending*

For completeness, in addition to the outward bending (that is the bending which "elongates" the sensible conductive layer), we performed the inward bending, in particular from 0° to -90°, 5° stepped, averaging data of ten iterations. As it can be expected, results demonstrated the uselessness of RFSs in inward flexion. As an example, Figure 12 reports the behavior of the C1 (polyester-coated 3" long) FP RFS sample.

This figure reports a non-monotonic function, which leads to the impossibility to determine unequivocally a bending angle from the reading of the resistance of the sensor. In addition, Figure 12 shows an inconsistent repeatability of the measure, since we obtained meaningful standard deviations (SDs), in particular for angle of bending within the -70° and 0° interval.

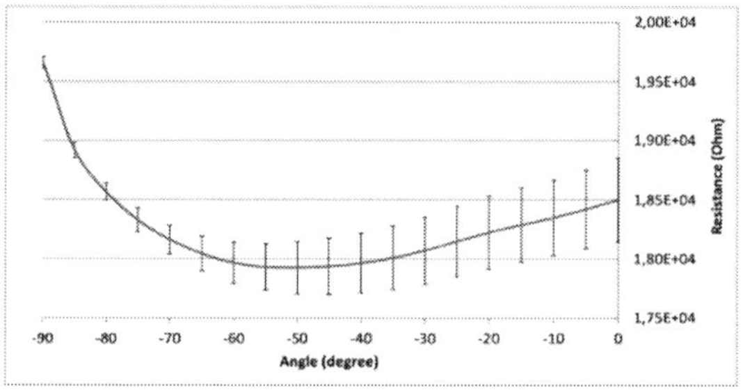

Figure 12. How FP C1 sample behves in inward bending. Vertical lines evidence high value of SD

G. *Step Response Decay*

A common requirement for any sensor is that its response has to be always the same with unchanging boundary conditions. In addition, a time-independent sensor has to maintain its response unchanged over time. In order to evaluate this characteristic for our RFSs, we tested their *step response decay* (a variation in resistance over time after a step transition to a different bending angle).

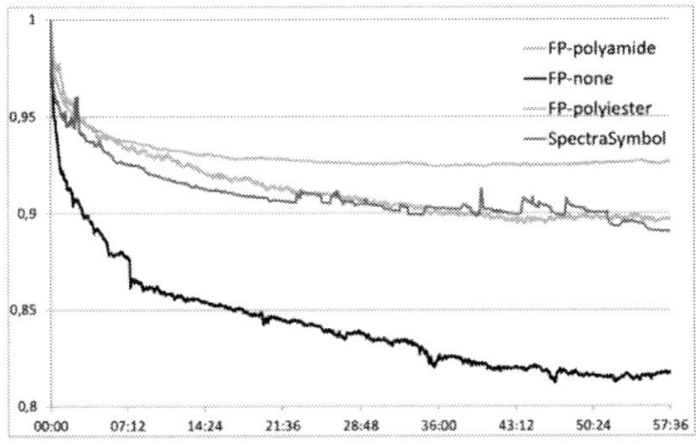

Figure 13. Step response decay, during 60min, for all RFSs under test.

Figure 13 reports the obtained results.

Approximately 15 mins are necessary for the FP polyamide-coated, for the FP polyester-coated and for the SS RFSs to gain a roughly stable value of resistance, respectively equal to the 93%, 90% and 90% of their initial value; a triple time (45mins) occurs for the FP bare RFS to reach some stability in resistance equal to the 82% of the initial value. These results are comparable to the ones obtained in [14], and suggest that it is fundamental to always establish the same acquisition time after each bending of the sensors.

IV. CONCLUSIONS

The choice of the right RFS is strictly related to the application.

The FP RFSs offer high sensitivity but low linearity within all the tested bending range (0°-120°). Such sensors are well exploited when connected to a low-gain non-linear amplifier. The fact that FP RFSs with the same characteristics (equal length and coating) behave differently, force the user to perform tests before their usage or, alternatively, to count on the normalized resistance values rather than the actual ones.

The coating reduces the sensitivity of the sensors, so that it can be recommended to use a coated sensor when strictly necessary, for example when RFSs have to be used in a harsh environment.

The SS RFSs offer high linearity but low sensitivity, so that are well exploited when connected to a high-gain linear amplifier. In addition, SS RFSs of the same type (here a unique one) behaves with the same resistance values, so that we can perform a unique test before their utilization.

High and acceptable repeatability of measurements was demonstrated for SS and FP RFSs respectively, and, for all RFSs, the importance to establish and maintain a time cadence in acquiring the measures to overcome issues related to the not-negligible step response decay.

All considering, the commercial RFSs we tested are suitable to be generally adopted as bending sensors.

ACKNOWLEDGMENT

This paper was partially based on a work supported by the Italian Space Agency (ASI), contract #2013-081-R0, for which we would like to thank Prof. Mariano Bizzarri, Dr. Simona Zoffoli and Dr. Francesca Ferranti.

REFERENCES

[1] G. Orengo, A. Lagati, G. Saggio, G. "Modeling Wearable Bend Sensor Behavior for Human Motion Capture." IEEE Sensors Journal, Volume: 14 , Issue: 7, pp. 2307 – 2316, 2014

[2] G. Saggio, F. Riillo, L. Sbernini, L . R. Quitadamo "Resistive flex sensors: a survey." Smart Materials and Structures, Volume 25, Number 1, pp. 1-30, 2016

[3] A. S. Evani, B. Sreenivasan, S. S. Joshi, M. Prakash, and J. Bapat, "Activity Recognition Using Wearable Sensors for Healthcare." In: The Seventh International Conference on Sensor Technologies and Applications, (Barcelona) pp 173-7, 2013

[4] D. A. Kingsley, R. D. Quinn and R. E. Ritzmann, "A cockroach inspired robot with artificial muscles." In: IEEE/RSJ International Conference on Intelligent Robots and Systems, (Beijing, China), pp 1837-42, 2006

[5] L. X. Ng, S. W. Oon, S. K. Ong and A. Y. C. Nee, "GARDE: a gesture-based augmented reality design evaluation system," International Journal on Interactive Design and Manufacturing (IJIDeM) 5 pp. 85-94, 2011

[6] L. Persson "Bältespåminnelse-system för baksäte: inventering och utvärdering." University West, Department of Technology, 2002

[7] L. C. Hau and K. D. Kincaid, "Method and apparatus for detecting a pedestrian impact." (Google Patents), 2008

[8] A. Mulder "Getting a GRIP on alternate controllers: Addressing the variability of gestural expression in musical instrument design" Leonardo music journal 6 pp. 33-40, 1996

[9] J. Bukhari, M. Rehman, S. I. Malik, A. M. Kamboh and A. Salman "American Sign Language Translation through Sensory Glove." SignSpeak International Journal of u-and e-Service, Science and Technology 8 pp. 131-42, 2015

[10] http://www.nicomatic.co.uk/pages/products/conductive%20compounds/c100.htm

[11] R. Gentner and J. Classen "Development and evaluation of a low-cost sensor glove for assessment of human finger movements" Neurophysiological settings Journal of neuroscience methods. pp. 178 138-47, 2009

[12] G. Orengo, A. Lagati, G. Saggio, "Bend Sensors Modeling for Fast Signal Recovering in Human Motion Analysis" The 3rd International Conference on Sensor Device Technologies and Applications, pp. 21-24, 2012

[13] G. Saggio "Mechanical model of flex sensors used to sense finger movements", Sensors and Actuators A 185, pp. 53– 58, 2012

[14] N. P. Oess, J. Wanek and A. Curt "Design and evaluation of a low-cost instrumented glove for hand function assessment" Journal of neuroengineering and rehabilitation, 2012

Intercomparisons of Inertial Heading Sensors: Reference Sensor with Zero Systematic Error

V. A. Granovskii and M. D. Kudryavtsev
Metrology services
Concern CSRI ELEKTROPRIBOR, JSC
St. Petersburg, Russia
e-mail: vgranovsky@eprib.ru, valgr39@mail.ru

***Abstract*—The paper formulates the problem of intercomparing inertial heading sensors to check if the tested sensor complies with the specified requirements. We show in this paper that the problem can be solved if the error of the reference sensor is known with sufficient accuracy. This study creates perspectives for solving the problem of calibration against the primary standard during marine tests of heading sensors.**

Keywords-sensor; heading sensor; inertial sensor; sensors intercomparison; sensor error; systematic error; random error

I. Introduction

Intercomparisons of inertial heading sensors are generally conducted to determine their corrections during pre-cruise preparation and to check their serviceability during operation [1]–[3]. These intercomparisons have two important features: first, more accurate sensors can be used for correction determination, and second, a small volume of data samples is available due to limited time of intercomparison.

Accuracy characteristics of the heading sensor during marine tests are traditionally determined by the same methods because we are supposed not to have heading standard at sea. By the latter we mean the device determining heading with an error negligibly small compared with the error of the tested sensor. Indeed, achieving a constant heading and keeping it does not solve the problem as the heading keeping accuracy is a fortiori lower than the required measurement accuracy (for successful intercomparison). Using Global Positioning System (GPS) data (if available) for heading calibration is usually impossible due to insufficient accuracy (with required update rate) or insufficient data rate (with required accuracy). Insufficient accuracy is even more degraded by the ship deformations, which make it impossible to install GPS receivers at the desired distance.

Thus, the heading sensor error is determined as follows during the tests: in static mode, the geodetic direction known to the desired accuracy is transferred to the ship, and the deviation between this direction and the direction of the sensor such as the axis of inertial trihedral formed by the heading sensor is determined. For higher reliability, the procedure is repeated before the ship goes to sea for marine tests and after its return. Clearly, in this case the heading sensor is not tested in the most complicated dynamic heading generation mode, during maneuvering in the open sea. At the same time, there are no obstructions for using a traditional metrological procedure of *intercomparison of measures* [4] to determine the heading accuracy.

This paper aims to demonstrate the possibility of checking the *tested heading sensor* (TS) by intercomparing it with another sensor further referred to as a *reference* (RS). In this paper, we assume that the RS generates heading with an error known to the required accuracy and without any systematic error. It is the set of two parameters – the ratio between the errors of the TS and RS, and the accuracy of estimating the RS error – which defines the test success. In the rest of the article we will refer of estimating both the systematic and random components of the TS error.

The rest of the paper is structured as follows. In Section II, we formulate the problem and, in Section III, we present the solution to the formal problem. The paper concludes in Section IV.

II. Problem Formulation

To reach this aim, the paper discusses the variants of the general problem of processing heading data generated by the intercompared sensors, which is formulated as follows.

As the heading sensors are installed onboard the ship, the physical (measured) heading axes of the TS and RS are aligned with the ship centerline plane accurate to Φ and Φ_{ref}, respectively. Thus, the relative offset of the axes is $\Delta\Phi = \Phi - \Phi_{ref}$ (see Fig. 1). Because of that, RS has zero systematic error, and we can ensure $\Phi_{ref} = 0$ by the special measuring procedure. So, it is supposed further that $\Delta\Phi = \Phi$, and, besides, Φ is significantly less than the error norm of TS. The general error model used in the paper is a random value with expected value (at start) presents a systematic error of a TS (denoting below by a). So we consider intercomparisons of a TS and RS where the latter has zero systematic error. As a rule, heading sensors error is characterized by *standard deviation* (denoting below by σ and σ_{ref}) or confidence limits. This paper mostly addresses normalization of standard deviation of random error (setting σ_{max} and $\sigma_{ref,\,max}$), and setting confidence limits is considered to be the secondary normalization method. During the tests, the sensors output current heading arrays $\{\varphi_i\}$ and $\{\varphi_{\mathrm{ref},\,i}\}$ at discrete time moments $\{t_i\}$, where $i = 1, \ldots, n$. The array volume n is determined by the test duration and sampling rate of digital signals (data readout rate). Usually, several runs are made during the tests, each being several hours long (up to 10–12 hours). The initial period of each run is occupied by the device thermal stabilization (and other kinds of stabilization). Thus, with sampling rate of the order of (1–100) Hz the volume of array n can reach several thousands and more.

It is supposed that the array data are generated synchronously, which makes it possible to generate the difference array $\{x_i\}$, where $x_i = \varphi_i - \varphi_{\mathrm{ref},\,i}$. Definitely, readings $\{\varphi_{\mathrm{ref},\,i}\}$ include information on the accuracy of RS, though in latent form, since true heading $\varphi_0 = \varphi_0(t)$ at each time t is unknown.

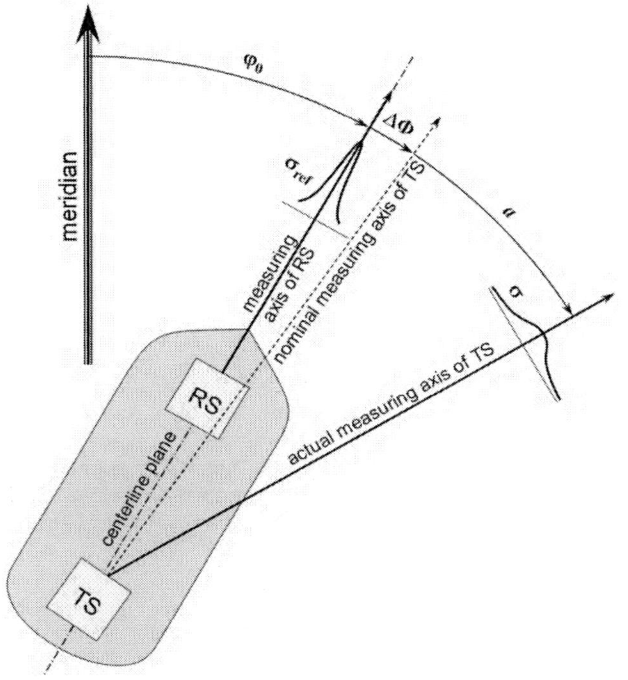

Figure 1. Measuring scheme of intercomparisons TS and RS.

Even if the design of RS provides zero heading systematic error, the ratio of spectra of sensor random error and true heading as a function of time generally remains unknown, which does not allow setting adequate averaging parameters for random error to find the true heading. Then, for a good RS, true σ_{ref} may turn out to be less than $\sigma_{\mathrm{ref,\,max}}$, however, since it is unknown, statistical conclusions about the TS based on the normative parameters of RS will be less reliable. True rather than normative parameters can be obtained using two methods. First, true parameters are determined during the installation of RS onboard the ship and after its repair, and are recorded in the sensor service log. Second, if the spectrum of true heading can be determined, one can try to estimate the variance of its random error component by filtering the low-frequency part. Keeping these possibilities in mind, further we suppose the normative parameter $\sigma_{\mathrm{ref,\,max}}$ to be rather close to the true value of σ_{ref}.

Clearly, the difference of readings x can be represented by symbolic sum of initial installation error $\Delta\Phi$ and the errors of intercompared sensors ξ, ξ_{ref}:

$$x = \Delta\Phi \oplus \xi \oplus \xi_{\mathrm{ref}}. \quad (1)$$

Equation (1) is the principal methodological basis of the test method by intercomparison TS with RS.

Further the array $\{x_i\}$ is considered to be a sample the of parent population generated by the sum of quasideterministic drift and ergodic stationary process modeling the sensor inaccuracy in steady mode. From the experience of development and operation of heading sensors, the drift nature of a certain device is assumed not to change from run to run. When modeling the drift by an exponential function, it means that the number of elements (power) of polynomial remains unchanged, and only its coefficients change. As to the stochastic part of this sum, assumption on its character requires thorough experimental check. The assumption is based on the fact that development and check-out of the device is a long multistep process aimed at stabilization of sensor construction in real operating conditions. As to the hypothesis of stationary stochastic part of the above mentioned sum, it relies on the assumption of sensor accuracy independency on the current heading (and its variations). This assumption, and therefore, stationarity hypothesis, requires verification. This verification is quite possible while the samples are large. The ergodicity hypothesis can be checked only partially (check of equality of ensemble and time averages) because of limited number of runs. At the same time, it should be emphasized that error time series can be treated as samples of the relevant parent populations on ergodicity assumption only.

Assuming that the data of the intercompared sensors received in each run after stabilization are analyzed, the elements of array $\{x_i\}$ can be considered to be the differences of random values ξ_i and $\xi_{\mathrm{ref},\,i}$ characterized by mathematical expectations a, a_{ref} and variances σ^2, σ_{ref}^2 (or standard deviations σ, σ_{ref}). It is supposed that the moments of each value ξ_i, $\xi_{\mathrm{ref},\,i}$ can change from run to run but remain unchanged within a run. Then due to large arrays of samples, sampling moments will practically coincide with the relevant probability characteristics, i.e., the moments of the considered parent populations.

We are not supposed to have information on spectral characteristics of errors of the intercompared sensors, firstly, the RS, thus, the ship true heading φ_0 cannot be determined by filtering the sensor readings.

Accuracy requirements on the TS are set as norms of statistical characteristics of its error. First of all, standard deviations σ and confidence limits ($a \pm K(P)\cdot\sigma$; P, F) are used, where P is the given confidence probability, F is the accepted probability distribution law. In practice, P=0.997 is often used, which corresponds to the confidence limits equal to the tripled standard deviation σ for symmetrical Gaussian distribution. In this case the problem of processing of data received by intercomparing the heading sensors is formulated as follows:

(*a*) by analyzing the array $\{x_i\}$, $i = 1, \ldots, n$ of difference of output signals φ_i and $\varphi_{\text{ref}, i}$ from the intercompared sensors determine, according to the substantiated criterion, whether actual standard deviation σ of the error of TS (or confidence limit) agrees with the required norm $\sigma_{\max}$ for the given data array (run);

(*b*) repeat (*a*) for all arrays (runs) and determine the maximum (worst) estimates of these parameters.

Therefore, further research is aimed to develop solution methods for the above given formal problem and its components.

This formal problem falls into several variants depending on a priori information on parameters of sensor data arrays. Here, we restrict ourselves to a practically significant case of a RS *without systematic component* in the error. The variants are presented in Table 1. Notation $a \in [a_{\text{low}}, a_{\text{up}}]$ means that sample average changes from run to run but remains unchanged within a run. Notation a = const means that the sample average remains unchanged also from run to run.

TABLE I. VARIANTS OF PROBLEM CONDITIONS

Variant	A priori information on parameters of		Analyzed parameters of		Note
	array $\{\varphi_{\text{ref}, i}\}$	array $\{\varphi_i\}$	RS	TS	
A	$a_{\text{ref}} = 0$	$a = 0$	σ_{ref}	σ	–
B	$a_{\text{ref}} = 0$	a = const	σ_{ref}	a, σ	–
C	$a_{\text{ref}} = 0$	$a \in [a_{\text{low}}, a_{\text{up}}]$	σ_{ref}	$a(j)$, σ	$j = 1, \ldots, m$ – run no.

Consider three combinations of parameters given in Table 1 step by the step using the same criteria.

III. SOLUTION OF THE FORMAL PROBLEM

A. *Random distortions of recorded signals only:* $a_{\text{ref}} = a = 0$

A1. To receive analytical solutions, with account for experience in studying the heading sensors, the character and volume of test data, and with account for the fact that any sampling moment is asymptotically normal [5], it would be expedient to use the following stochastic model with unbiased normal (Gaussian) distribution N of both sensor errors as a basic model:

$$\begin{cases} \varphi_{\text{ref}}(t) = \varphi_0(t) + \xi_{\text{ref}}(t), \;\; \xi_{\text{ref}}(t) \sim N(0, \sigma_{\text{ref}}^2) \text{ with any } t = t_i, \\ \varphi(t) = \varphi_0(t) + \xi(t), \;\; \xi(t) \sim N(0, \sigma^2) \text{ with any } t = t_i, \end{cases} \quad (2)$$

where σ_{ref} is the standard deviation of random error of RS (known); σ is the standard deviation of random error of TS (to be determined); $\varphi_0(t)$ is the unknown true heading at time t. The readings are supposed to be mutually noncorrelated: $\text{cov}[\xi(t), \xi_{\text{ref}}(t)] = 0$ with any $t = t_i$.

Under these conditions, the following is true for the variance $D_x = D[x(t)]$ of difference $x(t) = \varphi(t) - \varphi_{\text{ref}}(t)$ of readings of two intercompared sensors:

$$D_x = D[\xi(t) - \xi_{ref}(t)] = \sigma^2 + \sigma_{ref}^2 . \quad (3)$$

Expression (3) serves as a basis for the criterion to check whether true standard deviation of the TS error complies with the requirements. Determine the sample variance $\tilde{D}_x$ of differences $x_i = \varphi_i - \varphi_{\text{ref}, i}$ of sensor discrete readings:

$$\tilde{D}_x = \sum_{i=1}^{n} (x_i - \bar{x})^2 / (n-1) \quad (4)$$

where $\bar{x} = n^{-1} \cdot \Sigma x_i$, n is the sample size, and with account for its proximity to the parent population variance (3), compare it with the sum of norms for error variances taken as an acceptable upper estimate (4). If the given normative limit

$$\tilde{D}_x > \sigma_{\max}^2 + \sigma_{ref,\max}^2 \quad (5')$$

is exceeded, where $\sigma_{\max}$, $\sigma_{\text{ref, max}}$ are the norms of standard deviation of the TS and RS, the TS is known *bad*, while then definitely $\sigma > \sigma_{\max}$. However, to confirm the *fitness* of the TS (so that the inequality $\sigma \leq \sigma_{\max}$ is undeniably valid), this limit should be toughened while checking

$$\tilde{D}_x \leq \sigma_{\max}^2 + M^2 \cdot \sigma_{ref,\max}^2 , \quad (5'')$$

where coefficient $M = \inf\{\sigma_{\text{ref}} / \sigma_{\text{ref, max}}\} \leq 1$ determines the criterion "dead zone":

$$M < \frac{\sqrt{\tilde{D}_x - \sigma_{\max}^2}}{\sigma_{ref,\max}} \leq 1. \quad (5''')$$

This zone has a relative width $1-M$ and characterizes the acceptable risks of the manufacturer and the customer.

It should be also noted that criterion (5) is invariant to the type of error distribution, and in this sense is far beyond the framework of model (2). However, it ignores the possible random error of total estimated variance (4), and thus has a deterministic nature.

A more detailed criterion of sensor fitness can be based on setting the confidence limit for the module of error difference $|\Delta\xi|$ equal to the module of difference of readings from the intercompared sensors: $|\Delta\xi_i| = |\xi_i - \xi_{\text{ref}, i}| = |\varphi_i - \varphi_{\text{ref}, i}| = |x_i|$. While differences $\{x_i\}$ retain their Gaussian distribution in conditions of model (2), the confidence limit for $|\Delta\xi|$ is $\Delta_{conf} = 3\sqrt{\tilde{D}_x}$ (P=0.997), where $\tilde{D}_x$ is calculated by (4). Thus, in accordance with this criterion, the TS is considered *bad* if condition

$$n^+ > n(1-P) \quad (6')$$

holds, where n^+ is the number of "extreme" differences of samples x_i exceeding the acceptable limits

$$\pm 3\sqrt{\sigma_{\max}^2 + \sigma_{ref,\max}^2} . \quad (*)$$

Then, to rank the TS as *good* we should count the number $n^{++} > n^+$ of "extreme" differences of samples x_i exceeding the toughened limits

$$\pm 3\sqrt{\sigma_{\max}^2 + M^2 \cdot \sigma_{ref,\max}^2} , \quad (**)$$

where M is determined in (5″), and check if condition

$$n^{++} \leq n(1-P) \quad (6'')$$

is fulfilled.

It can easily be seen that the dead zone of this criterion is given by

$$n^{+} \le n(1-P) < n^{++} \qquad (6''')$$

and has a relative width $(n^{++} - n^{+})/[n(1-P)]$. Note that criterion (6) is highly sensitive to anomalous outliers in raw data.

A2. If it cannot be established that the TS error has a Gaussian distribution, and some interval $[-\Delta, \Delta]$ exists only which embraces its values, the following model should be used instead of model (2):

$$\begin{cases} \varphi_{ref}(t) = \varphi_0(t)+\xi_{ref}(t), \quad \xi_{ref}(t) \sim N(0, \sigma_{ref}^2) \text{ with any } t=t_i, \\ \varphi(t) = \varphi_0(t)+\xi(t), \quad \xi(t) \sim U(-\Delta, \Delta) \text{ with any } t=t_i, \end{cases} \qquad (2a)$$

where $U(-\Delta, \Delta)$ is the uniform distribution of TS errors, Δ is the limiting error module (which is to be estimated and should not exceed the given normative error Δ_{max}). This is justified because the error is set by its limits and uniform distribution is the worst variant of unimodal distributions [6]. Here, for the sake of uniformity of statistical methods in use, instead of Δ further we will consider equivalent standard deviation of uniform distribution $\sigma = \Delta/\sqrt{3}$ with the norm $\sigma_{max} = \Delta_{max} / \sqrt{3}$.

In this case, expressions (3)–(6) remain in force with relevant changes of coefficient K=3 for the standard deviations in (*), (**) through composition $N*U$ of distributions in model (2a) [5], [6].

A3. If the limits of RS error are specified, similarly to (2a) we have

$$\begin{cases} \varphi_{ref}(t) = \varphi_0(t)+\xi_{ref}(t), \ \xi_{ref}(t) \sim U(-\Delta_{ref}, \Delta_{ref}) \text{ with any } t=t_i, \\ \varphi(t) = \varphi_0(t)+\xi(t), \quad \xi(t) \sim N(0, \sigma^2) \text{ with any } t=t_i, \end{cases} \qquad (2b)$$

where $\sigma_{ref}=\Delta_{ref}/\sqrt{3}$ is known; σ is to be estimated. For this case, as well as above, modified formulas for the criteria (5)–(6) can be received through composition $N*U$.

A4. If there are no grounds to present the errors of both sensors using Gaussian distribution, uniform distribution should be used similar to models (2a) and (2b):

$$\begin{cases} \varphi_{ref}(t) = \varphi_0(t)+\xi_{ref}(t), \ \xi_{ref}(t) \sim U(-\Delta_{ref}, \Delta_{ref}) \text{ with any } t=t_i, \\ \varphi(t) = \varphi_0(t)+\xi(t), \quad \xi(t) \sim U(-\Delta, \Delta) \text{ with any } t=t_i, \end{cases} \qquad (2c)$$

where $\sigma_{ref}=\Delta_{ref}/\sqrt{3}$ is known; $\sigma=\Delta/\sqrt{3}$ is to be estimated. Here, modified formulas of criteria (5)–(6) can also be received through composition $U*U$.

Thus, in the considered cases, where the assumption on Gaussian distribution of random errors of intercompared sensors is not fulfilled, the solution to the formulated problem exists and can be received using formulas (3)–(6) or their simple modifications.

B. RS has random distortions only: $a_{ref} = 0$, and TS has both random and constant systematic signal distortions: $a = const$

By distortions, we mean inaccurate initial zero setting and constant error in certain runs of the TS, and if the data received in several runs are processed, a is considered to be constant from run to run. Thus, the following biased stochastic model with Gaussian error distribution is taken:

$$\begin{cases} \varphi_{ref}(t) = \varphi_0(t)+\xi_{ref}(t), \quad \xi_{ref}(t) \sim N(0,\sigma_{ref}^2) \text{ with any } t=t_i, \\ \varphi(t) = \varphi_0(t)+\xi(t), \quad \xi(t) \sim N(a,\sigma^2) \text{ with any } t=t_i, \end{cases} \qquad (2d)$$

where σ_{ref} is known, $\{a, \sigma\}$ are to be estimated on the assumption that the readings of intercompared sensors are noncorrelated: $cov[\xi_{ref}(t), \xi(t)]=0$ with any $t=t_i$. Then mathematical expectation a is not known, though its estimation is needed merely to estimate the standard deviation σ.

Obviously, in these assumptions for the variances the relation (3) is still valid. Then, while the bias a is constant, parameter D_x can be estimated by the same formula (4). It should be noted that criteria (5)–(6) can be modified with the account for these particular conditions.

Getting back to formula (4), note that the expression for $\bar{x}$ used in it is the estimate of the bias a of the TS. Thus, the confidence limits of its total error in this case are

$$\begin{cases} \Delta_{conf,low} = \bar{x} - K\sqrt{\tilde{D}_x - \sigma_{ref}^2} \\ \Delta_{conf,up} = \bar{x} + K\sqrt{\tilde{D}_x - \sigma_{ref}^2} \end{cases} \qquad (7)$$

with $K=K(P)=3$ for $P=0.997$ (in Gaussian case).

We can also apply standard methods to check the hypothesis of normal distribution of pairwise differences of samples $\{\varphi_{ref,i}\}$, $\{\varphi_i\}$, and with some rather general conditions for unknown signal $\varphi_0(t)$, of the samples themselves (after reasonable correction). For example, transformation to symmetrical first differences of each sample $\delta\varphi_{ref,i} = \varphi_{ref,i-1} - \varphi_{ref,i+1}$ and $\delta\varphi_i = \varphi_{i-1} - \varphi_{i+1}$ actually compensates the contribution of alternating signal $\varphi_0(t)$. Then their normal distribution (if such) will be maintained. The other method to suppress $\varphi_0(t)$ consists in calculating the symmetrical moving average (with a window of appropriate width) for each realization with further subtraction of the result. Samples corrected by this method (i.e., reduced to "zero" input signal) should be checked for normality.

Other than Gaussian error distributions can be considered similar to variants (*A2*)–(*A4*), and with relevant changes of coefficient K=3 for the standard deviations in (7).

C. RS has random distortions only: $a_{ref} = 0$, and TS has both random and constant systematic signal distortions, with the latter changing from run to run: $a \in [a_{low}, a_{up}]$.

If only the standard deviation σ is to be estimated, variant (*B*) should be repeated m times (with different a) and take the worst estimates by (4)–(6). If we are interested in total error, we search for confidence limits of the form $a \pm K(P) \cdot \sigma$ (also the worst among m runs), where $K(P)$ corresponds to the composition of the normal N and uniform U distributions (in various combinations $N*N$, $N*U$, $U*U$).

IV. CONCLUSIONS

Analysis and formulation of the problem of intercomparing an inertial heading sensor with some reference sensor to check the accuracy of the former show that the problem can be solved. Compliance or noncompliance of the tested sensor error to the specified norms can be reliably established. Traditional condition of sensors intercomparing has been analyzed and extended. We proceeded on the following assumptions: (a) the volume of an initial data (the sample size) under processing is large ($n \gg 1$); (b) the array data from the sensors are generated synchronously; (c) the normative parameter $\sigma_{ref,\ max}$ is rather close to true value of σ_{ref}; (d) the difference array $\{x_i\}$ is a sample of parent population generated by the sum of quasideterministic drift and ergodic stationary process; (e) the drift nature of a certain device is assumed not to change from run to run; (f) the moments of each value ξ_i, $\xi_{ref,\ i}$ can change from run to run but remain unchanged within a run; (g) the mathematical expectation of the reference sensor data equals zero; (h) the readings are supposed to be mutually noncorrelated: $cov[\xi(t), \xi_{ref}(t)]=0$ with any $t=t_i$; (j) all pairs of the popular stochastic models (Gaussian and uniform distributions) for the sensor data are considered.

It is shown that the problem can be solved in the presence of accurate estimate of characteristic of reference sensor error, particularly, the estimate close to the established accuracy norm. The obtained theoretical relationships and dependencies can serve as a basis for developing procedures for heading sensor intercomparisons, and under the defined conditions, solve the problem of calibration against the primary standard during marine tests of the heading sensors.

REFERENCES

[1] P. Manley, "Practical Navigation for the Modern Boat Owner," Wiley Nautical, 2008.

[2] "The American Practical Navigator: An Epitome of Navigation," Originally by N. Bowditch, LL.D., 1995 Ed. Bethesda, Maryland: National Imagery and Mapping Agency.

[3] ECOS Pilot School, postanite dio tradicije. "Practical Navigation Principles": www.ecos-psa.hr/practical-navigation-principles [retrieved: Mar. 2016].

[4] International vocabulary of metrology – Basic and general concepts and associated terms (VIM), 3rd ed. Joint Committee for Guides in Metrology, 2012.

[5] H. Cramér, "Mathematical methods of statistics". Uppsala: Almqvist and Wiksells, 1945.

[6] S. G. Rabinovich, "Measurement errors and uncertainties: theory and practice" – 2nd ed. N.Y.: Springer-Verlag, 2000.

Using Customized Computer Vision and Charge-Coupled Device (CCD) Sensor for the Recognition of Colony Formation and Counting of Live Bacteria in the Agricultural Industry

Gabriel M. Alves
Federal University of São Carlos
Embrapa Instrumentation
São Carlos, SP, Brazil
e-mail: gabriel.alves@dc.ufscar.br

Paulo E. Cruvinel
Embrapa Instrumentation
Federal University of São Carlos
São Carlos, SP, Brazil
e-mail: paulo.cruvinel@embrapa.br

***Abstract*—This paper presents an arrangement based on a customized computer and Charge-Coupled Device (CCD) sensor system to allow the counting and recognition of the colony formation, in an intelligent manner, of live bacteria. Microbes in agricultural environments are important catalysts of global carbon and nitrogen cycles, including the production and consumption of greenhouse gases in soil. The magnitude of this process is influenced by human activities and impacts the warming potential of Earth's atmosphere. The method implemented uses techniques of digital image processing, and among them, Hough Transform for circular objects. For calibration and validation of the method, a RGB (Red-Green-Blue) camera based on the CCD was used, as well as a prepared illuminated chamber, to allow the analysis of the bacteria *Escherichia Coli* and *Acidithiobacillus ferrooxidans*. The visual environment, Borland Builder C++, was used for the development, and a modeling for decision making was incorporated to aggregate intelligence. Moreover, a set of comparisons was established, taking into account the smart methods and analyses carried out by experts. The results have shown the potentiality of the method, which is applied for laboratory applications that involve the quantification and the pattern recognition of bacterial colonies in solid culture environments.**

Keywords-intelligent sensing; bacterial colonies counting; Hough Transform; computer vision.

I. Introduction

Some bacteria have properties that are beneficial to plants. They can be found in the soil, and they have the potentiality to affect, in a good way, the plants and cultures by fighting against the harmful bacteria. Also, they can be the source of providing nutrition to the crops. For instance, bacteria increase the fertility of the soil and provide nutrients, which are useful for plant growth. However, it is still open for research to better understand the role bacteria play when the plant grows. Although the cultivation of microorganisms in solid culture is a traditional technique, it continues being the compulsory step when it is necessary for the isolation and purification bacterium lines. Nowadays, the microbiology technique has been employed associated with the traditional techniques, including counting and cultivation in solid ways, when intending to quantify or isolate different groups of microorganisms.

Many institutes, laboratories and entities are concerned with establishing procedures, criteria and standards of microbiology analysis involving the counting of colonies in solid culture. The Ministry of Agriculture, Livestock and Food Supply, through the Normative Instruction nº 62, of August, 26 of 2003, established a procedure to standardize the counting of microorganism with application of samples of raw material, water and meals [1]. The National Agency of Health Surveillance (ANVISA) and the National Advice of Environment [2] are examples of worried entities with the criteria and standards of microbiology analyses.

There are different laboratory methods for counting bacteria. Among them, one may consider the Counting Chambers, which can fill in an automatic way a certain volume and uses a special microscope slide with a cover glass to calculate the number of bacteria per milliliter of the original sample from the known volume:the Most Probable Number, which estimates the number of bacteria; the Membrane Filters, in which the water is filtered on a filter which has holes smaller than bacteria and then is placed on a dish of agar, and bacteria grow on the top of the filter to be count; Photometers and Spectrometers, in which a meter reads the amount of light passing through the culture, and by consulting a standard curve which you have prepared by reading the meter and plating the bacteria, you can estimate the number of bacteria. These methods have the limitations of counting live and dead bacteria [3]-[11]. On the other hand, as a process of structural colony formation, which excludes dead bacteria and debris an opportunity is observed to have a method that uses a sensor for imaging and a computer aided system for pattern recognition and counting in an intelligent manner of the colony formation of live bacteria.

However, it has been observed that the manual counting of colonies is limited, because is a slow process and the number of analyses performed depends of visual exposure activity by the technician. Besides, in this context, the development of a method based on the use of a sensor which allows imaging for intelligent analysis of the colonies formation of the bacteria and automatic counting of the colonies formation units can speed up the number of laboratorial analyses.

This paper presents a system for the recognition of colonies formation of live bacteria and its counting. The method uses the Hough Transform, adapted for the detection of colonies with circular shapes, in order to aggregate the intelligence for decision making in the agricultural industry.

After this introduction, Section 2 presents the theoretical and technological background; Section 3 presents the method of aggregation of computer intelligence. Finally, the results and discussions are presented in Section 4, followed by the conclusion in Section 5.

II. Theoretical and Technological Background

A. Microbial growth phases

Most bacteria under optimal growing conditions grow and divide every half hour [12]. Thus, the increase in the population numbers from a single bacterium can be expressed as a geometric progression, as follows:

$$1 - 2^1 - 2^2 - 2^3 - \cdots - 2^n \quad (1)$$

where the exponent $(0, 1, 2, 3, \cdots n)$ refers to the number of generations. The time interval required for each microorganism to divide, or for the population of a culture to double in number, is known as generation time [13]. It should be noted that not every species of microorganisms have the same generation time. Fig. 1 illustrates the bacterial growth curve and its phases.

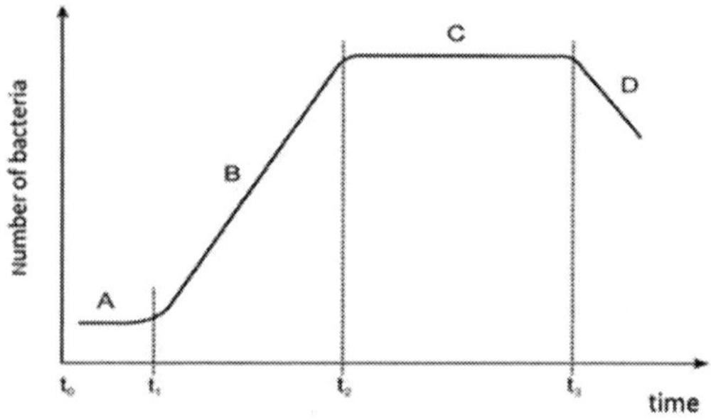

Figure 1. The phases of the bacteria growth: A - lag phase;B - exponential phase; C - stationary phase;D - declining phase (adapted from [12]).

There are four stages of growth that characterize the bacterial growth curve: lag phase, exponential phase, stationary phase and decline phase or cell death. Table I helps the understanding of the phases of bacteria growth, i.e., Figure 1, where each phase represents the notion in relation to its growing status.

TABLE I. The microbial growth phases.

Lag phase	$t_0 \leq t < t_1$
Exponential phase	$t_1 \leq t < t_2$
Stationary phase	$t_2 \leq t < t_3$
Declining phase	$t \geq t_3$

The lag phase occurs after the inoculation medium. The cells begin to adjust to the physical condition and available nutrients. During this time, the cells are in a latency period where there is an intense metabolic activity that is not reflected in the increase in cell number. This phase can continue for one hour to several days.

In the exponential phase, all cells are divided at regular intervals of time, resulting in an exponential increase in the number of individuals in the population. This phase is the period of high metabolic activity of the cell; however, the organisms are particularly sensitive to environmental changes.

The stationary phase occurs when the growth rate slows down and strikes a balance between the rate of death and the rate of divisions in the population.

Finally, the decline phase, or cell death, occurs when the rate of death exceeds the rate of divisions. This phase continues until the population disappears completely.

B. Manual Counting Method by Experts

The method based on manual analysis, employed in this work for comparison purposes with the automated method, uses a device which has a reticulated and illuminated acrylic surface wherein the Petri dish is placed, and above the surface, there is as increased magnifying 1.5 times with a flexible rod that allows the experts to visually count the existing bacteria colonies on the plate. For this research, the experts used an apparatus named Colony Counter Phoenix Luferco, model CP-608.

C. Sensor and Illumination System

A CCD camera is a semi-conductor device that acts as a transducer between incoming light and electrical charge. For the CCD sensor operation, it is important to consider the level of the environmental illumination in relation to the object one is going to work with. The lighting is an important factor to be considered in forming the image, as it can influence the final result of analysis, since the level of the pixel intensity will be a function of the illumination and the angle of its incidence over the object during the image acquisition process.

In systems for the automatic counting of colonies, generally, the main difficulty is the lighting system that requires high power lamps to be dimmer; in some cases, the use of special lenses or a combination of all these components is necessary. There are at least two methods of lighting that can be employed in an imaging system for bacteria counting. One is the method that uses backlight, and the second one is the method that uses front lighting. In the first method, the Petri dish is placed on a light source under the CCD camera. Generally, this method uses a white acrylic plate between the light source and the plate to produce a more uniform lighting. In the second, front lighting method, the Petri dish is placed below both the light source and the CCD camera. The camera captures the light of the environment and performs the registration of the frames for processing.

In order to get a better arrangement, for this research, a front lighting system was developed for the acquisition of the information from the bacterial colonies, which were located into Petri dishes. For the lighting system four fluorescent lamps of 20 watts connected by two electrical ballasts were used. The use of electrical ballasts avoided the effect of the flicker of the fluorescent lamps, which can be captured by the CCD cameras, i.e., generated undesirable noise. The box surrounding the set of bulbs was produced in wood. The box that packages the lamps and the Petri dish has the following internal measurements: 500 mm long by 250 mm wide and 500 mm in height. It has a front cover that allows the manipulation of samples and a top cover that closes the box. Internally there is a support for the lights and the camera (Fig. 3). The CCD involves that photons striking a silicon surface create free electrons through the photoelectric effect [14][15]. Nature abhors a vacuum and, thus, a concomitant positive charge (called as a hole) is generated, as well. If nothing else is done, the hole and the electron will recombine and release energy in the form of heat. This is accomplished by positively biasing discrete areas to attract electrons generated while the photons come onto the surface. The substrate of a CCD is made of silicon, but this is not where most of the action occurs. Photons coming from above the gate strike the epitaxial layer and generate photoelectrons. The gate is held at a positive charge in relation to the rest of the device, which attracts the electrons to it. Because of the insulating layer the electrons can't make it through to the gate and are held in place by the positive charge above them.

Fig. 2 shows a basic diagram of a CCD and the arrangement used for the serial image frame readout mode. The image acquisition process starts when the incoming photons reach the sensitive sensor array. To readout, the sensor of the accumulated charge must then be shifted vertically row by row into the serial output register. Besides, for each row the readout register must be shifted horizontally to allow for readout of each individual pixel.

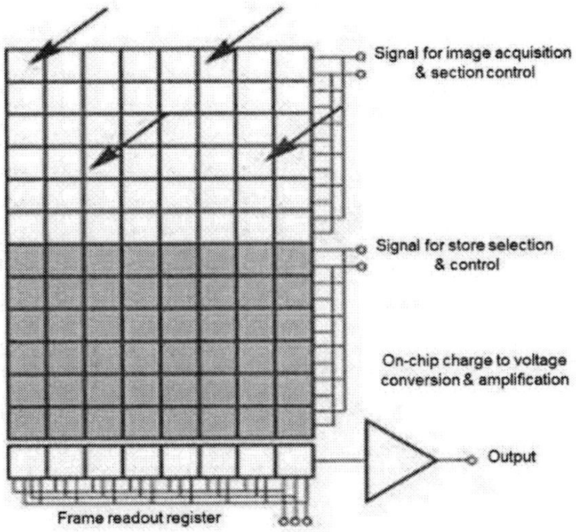

Figure 2. Block diagram of a CCD and its arrangement for the serial frame readout mode.

The serial shift is performed from top to bottom and directs the electron packets to the measurement electronics, which involve an analog to digital (A/D) converter to allow the measurement of the voltage created by the packet of electrons at the serial output and turn this into an electronic number that can then be digitally transmitted to and saved by a computer.

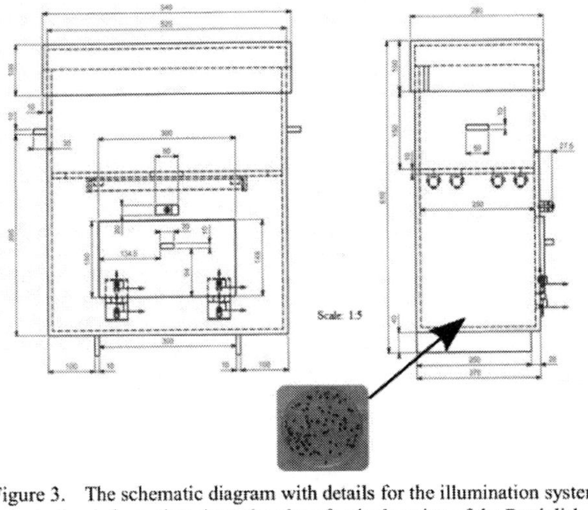

Figure 3. The schematic diagram with details for the illumination system, including information about the place for the location of the Petri dish, which is used for colonies bacteria growing.

In this schematic diagram, the following components of the illumination system are displayed: a box, the top cover, the front cover and built-in bracket for the lights and the CCD camera. Moreover, the arrow indicates that the Petri dish with the colonies is placed on the bottom center of box under electrical ballasts.

D. Hough Transform

The Hough Transform (HT) has been proposed as a method for detection of complex patterns in binary images by Paul Hough in 1962 in the form of a patent [16]. One of the goals Hough predicting was a method to recognize complex patterns in pictures; another goal was to provide a method and improved means for the recognition of particle tracks in photographs taken in a bubble chamber. The Hough Transform was first used in computer vision to detect parametric curves [16][17] and, more recently, for the widespread detecting of non-parametric forms [18][19].

In terms of circular objects, Duda and Hart (1972) suggested the use of the Hough Transform adapted circles. Whereas, the transform can be applied in the recognition curves, provided that the same can be described in parametric form are a circle may be provided by a parametric equation are that it is possible to adapt the Hough Transform for circles.

The property first defined that a point in the cartesian plane corresponds to a sine curve in the plane parameter. Extending this property, you can adapt it for circumference. In this case, a point on the cartesian plane corresponds to a circle in plan parameters. Thus, taking all the pixels of the cartesian plane and applying the circumference equation to have each pixel generate a circumference in the parameter space is represented by an accumulator array.

The parameter space is generated from the transformation of the Cartesian plane through the circular Hough Transform, where image points correspond to circles within the parameter and, therefore, the *a* and *b* coordinates are stored in the accumulator array. The crossing of the circumferences and the accumulated value in this cell defines how many pixels belong to the circle. Besides, the use of the technique known as backmapping provides means to reduce the false peaks, which are usually found in the Hough Transform [20]. In this work, we used a three dimensional accumulator array, in which a third dimension, representing the possible radii of circumference, can be detected. In this way, the definition of the new arrangement should be obtained by:

$$\sum_{y}^{Y_{max}} \sum_{x}^{X_{max}} \sum_{r=R_{min}}^{R_{max}} array(a,b,r) = \begin{cases} 1, if\ f(x,y) = 255 \\ 0, otherwise \end{cases} \qquad (2)$$

where $array(a,b,r)$ is the accumulator arrangement filled by Hough Transform, Y_{max} is the height of the image, X_{max} is the width of the image, r is the radius of the pattern to be recognized in the interval $[R_{min}, R_{max}]$, $a = x - \cos(\theta)$, $b = y - \sin(\theta)$, and $f(x,y)$ is the gray level of a pixel on the (x,y) coordinate whose value is in the range from 0 to 255.

The dimensions of the accumulator arrangement should be defined to avoid loss information, and it can be the same height and width of image. However, if one pixel on the image is near to the edge, the circle drawn exceed the limits in the arrangement. Thus, to avoid loss of information the dimensions of the accumulator array is defined by:

$$array[X_{max} + 2 * radius][Y_{max} + 2 * radius] \qquad (3)$$

where $radius$ means a value between interval $[R_{min}, R_{max}]$, Y_{max} is the height and X_{max} is the width of the image.

III. THE AGGREGATION OF COMPUTER INTELLIGENCE

The aggregation of intelligence was based on the use of a customized computer with 256MBytes of RAM, 1GHz processors, and a Windows© operational system. The algorithm to aggregate the decision-support system was developed using the object-oriented programming language C++. Additionally, the tool platforms were based on the Borland© C++ Builder. The flowchart of the algorithm is illustrated in Fig. 4 and consists of five modules, namely as: acquiring information module; pre-processing module; processing module; post processing module; module for analysis and decision making support.

The acquisition module includes a lighting system developed in order to maintain uniformity in luminance to obtain the process of capturing images suitable for analysis. The capture is achieved by means of a CCD sensor for higher pixel counts and miniaturization. The ICX452AQ, having a diagonal 9.04 mm (Type 1/1.8) 5.13M pixel, was used to respond to these needs, i.e., unit cell size equal to 2.775 μm (Horizontal) × 2.775 μm (Vertical) square pixels.

The pre-processing module contains a set of techniques to prepare the information collected from the bacteria for processing and is responsible for preparing to organize in a matrix to the stage of processing. This set includes a simple global threshold [21], the threshold of Otsu [22][23], conversion of color images (RGB) to shades of gray levels and detection of edges using the Laplacian filter [24][25].

The processing module uses circular Hough Transform to detect circular bacterial colonies from the pre-processed image, containing the edges of possible bacterial colonies with a circular primitive, and for each edge pixel, a circumference is generated and stored in the accumulator array.

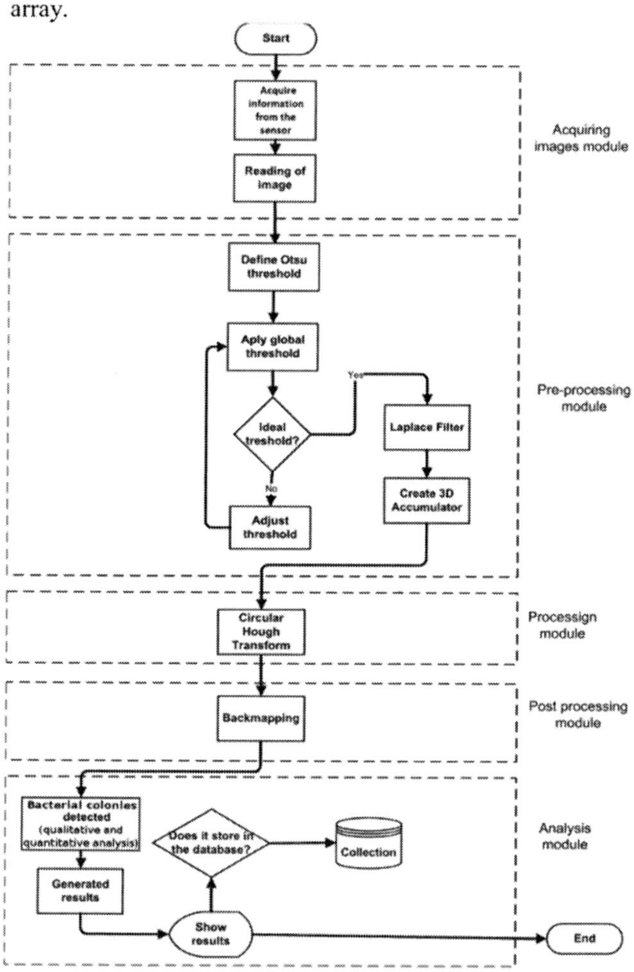

Figure 4. Flowchart of the algorithm which allows the aggregation of intelligence to support decision makers.

The post-processing stage is responsible for preparing the processed image for analysis and generation of results. The technique of backmapping is applied to the circular Hough Transform, i.e., in order to remove possible noise due to false peaks generated during the processing process.

Fig. 5 shows the class diagram for the sensor reading and computational vision and intelligence aggregation for the recognition of the formation and colony count of live bacteria.

The `CHoughCircle` generates and fills accumulator array implemented by `CMatrix` class. The `CSensor` is responsible for acquiring the image from the CCD sensor and preparing it for analysis. The `CFilter` class implements the essential functions to the automated method as laplacian filter.

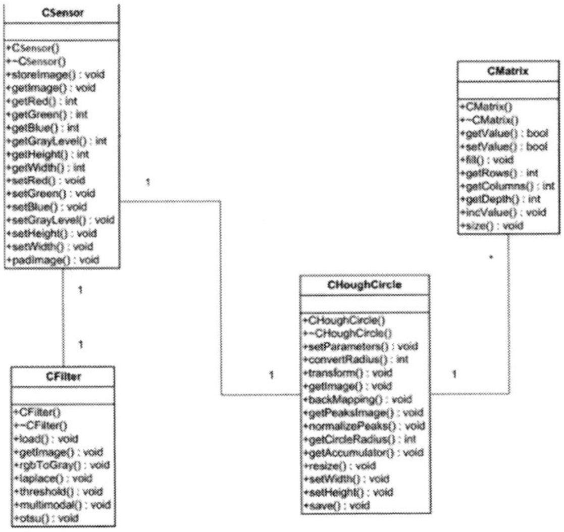

Figure 5. The class diagram of the system for counting the colony formation of live bacteria in an intelligent manner.

Furthermore, there is a stage for the analysis and decision making support that allows for extracting the number of the count and colony formation of live bacteria from the processed image. Information can also be extracted and stored in a collection for post-analysis of the growth of bacterial species.

IV. Results and Discussions

The illumination system allowed for regular illuminance of 1200 lumen/m² over the image. Outside, the 750 lumen/m² was the illuminance observed. Fig. 6 shows Petri dish information acquired, i.e., having bacteria in both cases, that means, inside and outside the illumination system and their respective histograms. The value of illuminance does not depend on the material properties of the surface being illuminated. However, since the information depends on how much is being reflected from other surfaces around it, it does depend on the color and reflectance of the surfaces that surround it.

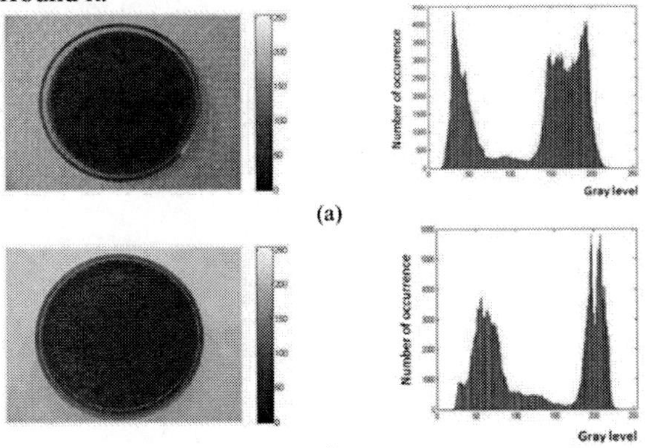

(b)

Figure 6. Culture of *Escherichia Coli*. (a) Information acquired in 256 gray levels without additional illumination and respective histogram. (b) Information acquired in 256 gray levels with additional illumination and respective histogram.

A set of twenty-six samples having bacteria was analyzed and divided into two groups, i.e., Group #1 and Group #2. For each group, computational and manual analysis was performed by experts. The values of absolute error, relative error and percentage error were calculated for each analyzed sample. The Fig. 7 shows the sample #22 of the Group #1, i.e., having *Escherichia Coli* samples.

Figure 7. Example of a sample prepared with *Escherichia Coli* from the Group #1. The white circles have show the processed information with the detected colonies (Above, on the left side, one may find the commands <file>, <image>, and <help>; on the right side, one may find, from top to the bottom, the fields for setting the parameters for analysis: initial radius, final radius, angle variation, background color selection (black or white), and also the command for <Application of the Hough Transform> and <Histogram>. Additionally, the number of reached colonies of bacteria/sample is also shown in the interface).

The results obtained with the smart method for the identification and colony count of the bacteria or even microorganisms identified 460 colonies, while for this exampled sample, the manual count realized by experts identified 472 colonies. Table II presents the results for the analysis carried out for Group #1, which had five samples of the bacteria *Escherichia coli* in the solid culture.

TABLE II. RESULTS OF THE ANALYSIS OF SAMPLES HAVING THE BACTERIA *Escherichia coli* IN SOLID CULTURE.

Sample #	Absolute error	Manual error		Smart method error	
		Relative	%	Relative	%
22	12.00	0.03	2.54	0.03	2.61
23	14.00	0.04	3.72	0.03	3.87
24	40.00	0.08	7.78	0.08	8.44
25	9.00	0.04	4.31	0.05	4.50
26	109.00	0.17	17.41	0.21	21.08

For this Group #1, one may observe that the percentage error was smaller than 10%, except for sample # 26, for which the error rate exceeded such percentage. However, it is possible to observe that the number of colonies per sample was greater than 300 in most cases and, for the smart method of counting, the errors remained small.

Fig. 8 shows the result of values dispersion, and the linear correlation coefficient was equal to 0.98, i.e., when plotting results obtained by measurements realized by experts versus those obtained with the smart method.

This graph presented in Fig. 8 shows that the absolute errors, which are associated with error-bars, are low in the majority of the measurements. In the sample which the error rate was greater than 10%, number of colonies were higher than 600. In such cases, the manual analysis by experts is usually performed by estimation of the occupied area on the plate and not actually counted, and such situation may explain these results.

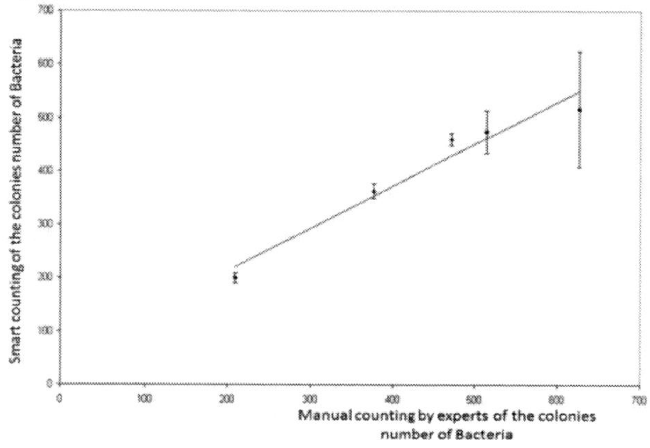

Figure 8. Correlation between the sensor-based recognition method and the manual by experts for the Group #1,which represents the *Escherichia coli* samples.

The contamination by *Escherichia coli* can be very complex and involves all aspects of human and the agricultural production, products and their interactions with ecosystem. The epidemiology of each pathotype varies with the reservoir host, levels of community sanitation and hygiene, and agriculture and food production systems. Prevention and control require a multidisciplinary approach in which the transducers and sensors, as well as intelligent systems and computer vision, plays an important role to evaluate the risk-based approaches and to support decision makers, i.e. involving from the producers up to the consumers. Group #2 of samples referred to the cultivation of *Acidithiobacillus ferrooxidans* on solid culture. Fig. 9 illustrates one of the results obtained with the intelligent counting process. For this exampled sample, the manual count by experts identified 82 colonies, while by the automatic method, the result returned 84 colonies for such sample.

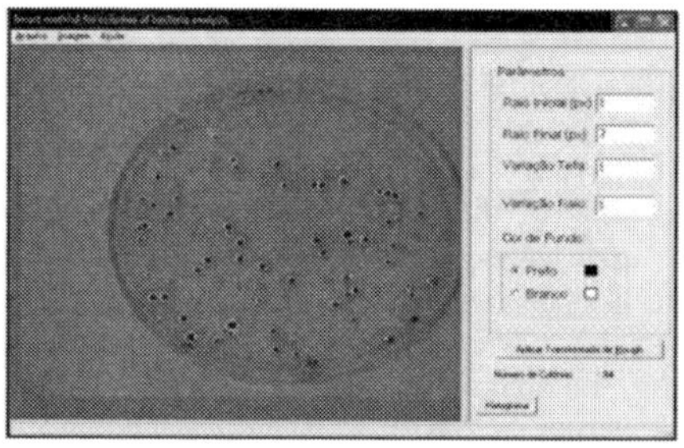

Figure 9. An example of one sample with the cultivation of the *Acidithiobacillus ferrooxidans*. The white circles have show the processed information with the detected colonies (Above, on the left side, one may find the commands <file>, <image>, and <help>; on the right side, one may find, from top to the bottom, the fields for setting the parameters for analysis: initial radius, final radius, angle variation, background color selection (black or white), and also the command for <Application of the Hough Transform> and <Histogram>. Additionally, the number of reached colonies of bacteria/sample is also shown in the interface).

Table III presents results, which were performed with the Group #2, having 21 samples prepared with the *Acidithiobacillus ferrooxidans* on solid culture. In this table the absolute, relative and percentage error found for each sample are presented.

TABLE III. RESULTS OF THE ANALYSIS OF SAMPLES HAVING THE BACTERIA *ACIDITHIOBACILLUS ferrooxidans* IN SOLID CULTURE.

Sample #	Absolute error	Manual error		Smart method error	
		Relative	%	Relative	%
1	2.00	0.02	2.44	0.02	2.38
2	1.00	0.02	1.52	0.02	1.54
3	6.00	0.11	10.71	0.12	12.00
4	3.00	0.08	8.33	0.09	9.09
5	1.00	0.02	2.38	0.02	2.44
6	3.00	0.03	2.63	0.03	2.56
7	1.00	0.01	0.77	0.01	0.76
8	10.00	0.18	17.86	0.15	15.15
9	3.00	0.04	4.17	0.04	4.00
10	2.00	0.02	2.44	0.03	2.50
11	1.00	0.02	2.27	0.02	2.22
12	5.00	0.03	2.86	0.03	2.78
13	1.00	0.02	2.13	0.02	2.08
14	1.00	0.01	1.06	0.01	1.05
15	21.00	0.10	9.50	0.11	10.50
16	17.00	0.12	11.89	0.13	13.49
17	3.00	0.07	7.14	0.07	6.67
18	12.00	0.06	6.32	0.06	5.94
19	2.00	0.06	5.71	0.05	5.41
20	4.00	0.05	5.48	0.05	5.19
21	4.00	0.07	7.41	0.07	6.90

From analysis of the Group #1, one may observe that the absolute error remained smaller than 10%. However, there are results which show a relative error rate above 10%, particularly sample #3, sample #8, sample #15, and sample #16. These results are linked to external factors inherent in the process of sample preparation. Examples of external factors of errors occur due to the provision of culture medium on the Petri dish that can face problems related with wrinkle or bubble, i.e., may find the growing of the colonies near the edge of the plate. Fig. 10 shows the result of dispersion of the values found in both the manual by experts and the automatic counting for Group #1.

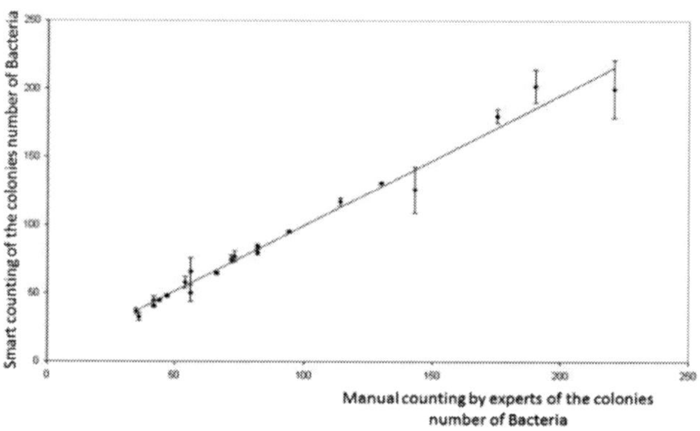

Figure 10. Correlation between the sensor-based recognition method and the manual by experts for the Group #1, which represents the *Acidithiobacillus ferrooxidans* samples.

In the graph, the bars of errors are associated with the absolute errors of each sample. The coefficient of linear correlation found was equal to 0.99. For this group, the number of colonies per sample was smaller than 200, and in this case, the results obtained by automatic analysis were very close to the manual one.

The Sulfur (S (symbol), Z (atomic number) = 16, ρ (density) = $2.07 g/m^3$) deficiency in soils is becoming common in many areas of the world, as a result of agricultural practices. Therefore, the development of a smart method to support decision making, especially in the processes related to the identification and count of colonies of microorganisms in soils, in particular those of the genus *Thiobacillus*, is very much required.

V. CONCLUSION

The method presented allowed intelligent recognition and both the qualitative analysis and the quantitative count of the bacteria colonies, i.e., using a customized computer and a CCD sensor, as well as the Hough Transform for circular microorganisms.

Groups of samples were analyzed to get the information regarding to the bacterial colonies growing, its formation and its number in the solid culture, all prepared in Petri dishes. Results have shown high linear correlation, i.e., when compared with the manual analysis executed by expert people. In both cases, the linear correlation coefficients were equal to 0.99, i.e., for the *Escherichia coli* samples (Group #1), and for the *Acidithiobacillus ferrooxidans* samples (Group #2), respectively.

In the future, based on qualitative and quantitative analysis on the bacteria and its colonies, additional methods will be designed and that will have the possibility to be used directly in the agricultural field for in-situ analyses. Additionally, this method will be able to be embedded and ported to Android smartphones for online processing.

ACKNOWLEDGMENT

The authors would like to thank Embrapa Instrumentation (CNPDIA), the Department of Computer Science from the Federal University of São Carlos (UFSCar) and the Federal Institute of Education, Science and Technology of São Paulo (IFSP) for their support in this work.

REFERENCES

[1] MAPA, "Ministry of agriculture, livestock and food supply. Normative Instruction n 62 (original in portuguese language)," 2003.

[2] CONAMA, "National Health Surveillance Agency, in the DRC 275: Technical regulation of microbiological characteristics for natural mineral water and natural water (original in portuguese language)," 2005.

[3] W. K. Durfee, "Designing smart machines.- teaching mechatronics to mechanical engineers through a project based, creative design course," Mechatronics, vol. 5, 1995, pp. 775–785.

[4] B. F. Spencer, M. E. Ruiz-Sandoval, and N. Kurata, "Smart sensing technology: opportunities and challenges," Structural Control and Health Monitoring, vol. 11, no. 4, 2004, pp. 349–368.

[5] M. C., J. E. Cohen, H. Setl, J. Bloem, and A. M. Breure, "Bacterial traits, organism mass, and numerical abundance in the detrital soil food web of dutch agricultural grasslands," Ecology Letters, vol. 8, 2005, pp. 80–90.

[6] F. O. Bendez´u and P. A. J. de Boer, "Conditional Lethality, Division Defects, Membrane Involution, and Endocytosis in mre and mrd Shape Mutants of Escherichia coli," Journal of Bacteriology, vol. 190, no. 5, March 2008, pp. 1792–1811. [Online]. Available: http://dx.doi.org/10.1128/JB.01322-07

[7] H. Ates and O. N. Gerek, "An image-processing based automated bacteria colony counter," 24th International Symposium on Computer and Information Sciences, 2009, pp. 18–23.

[8] S. Kothari, Q. Chaudry, and M. Wang, "Automated cell counting and cluster segmentation using concavity detection and ellipse fitting techniques," IEEE International Symposium on Biomedical Imaging: From Nano to Macro, 2009, pp. 795–798.

[9] M. Park, J. Jin, Y. Peng, P. Summons et al., "Automatic cell segmentation in microscopic color images using ellipse fitting and watershed," IEEE/ICME International Conference on Complex Medical Engineering, 2010, pp. 69–74. [Online]. Available: http://dx.doi.org/10.1109/ICCME.2010.5558869

[10] R. Hazan, Y.-A. Que, D. Maura, and L. G. Rahme, "A method for high throughput determination of viable bacteria cell counts in 96-well plates," BMC Microbiology, vol. 12, no. 1, 2012, pp. 1–7. [Online]. Available: http://dx.doi.org/10.1186/1471-2180-12-259

[11] G. M. Alves, P. E. Cruvinel, and H. A. F. Nascimento, "Automated method for cfu counting in petri dishes," Revista SODEBRAS, vol. 9, no. 101, May 2014, pp. 44–49.

[12] L. R. Trabulsi and M. R. F. Toledo, Microbiologia, 2nd ed. Rio de Janeiro: Editora Atheneu, 1991.

[13] M. J. J. Pelczar, E. C. S. Chan, and N. R. Krieg, Microbiologia: Conceitos e aplicac¸o˜es, 2nd ed. Pearson Education do Brasil, 1997, vol. 1, traduc¸a˜o Sueli Fumie Yamada, Tania Ueda Nakamura, Benedito Prado Dias Filho; revis˜ao t´ecnica Celso Vataru Nakamura.

[14] J. Mullikin, L. Vliet, H. Netten, F. Boddeke et al., "Methods for CCD camera characterization," Proc. SPIE Conference (San Jose CA, Febr.9-10, 1994), SPIE, vol. 2173, 1994, pp. 73–84.

[15] D. G. Abdelsalam, M. Stanislas, and S. Coudert, "CCD or CMOS camera calibration using point spread function," Proc. SPIE 9234, International Conference on Experimental Mechanics 2013 and Twelfth Asian Conference on Experimental Mechanics, 2014, pp. 92 340Z–92 340Z–4. [Online]. Available: http://dx.doi.org/10.1117/12.2048991

[16] P. V. C. Hough, "Method and means for recognizing complex patterns," 1962, u.S.Patent 3.069.654.

[17] R. O. Duda and P. E. Hart, "Use of the Hough transformation to detect lines and curves in pictures." Graphics and Image Processing, vol. 15, no. 1, 1972, pp. 11–15.

[18] M. Smereka and I. D. Eba, "Circular object detection using a modified hough transform," Int. J. Appl. Math. Comput. Sci., vol. 18, no. 1, 2008, pp. 85–91.

[19] B. Gorte and G. Sithole, "Lookup table hough transform for real time range image segmentation and featureless co-registration," Journal of Sensor Technology, vol. 2, no. 3, 2012, pp. 148–154.

[20] G. Gerig and F. Klein, "Fast Contour Identification through Efficient Hough Transform and Simplified Interpretation Strategy." IEEE, New York, NY, USA, 1986, pp. 498–500, cited By 47. [On-line]. Available: http://www.scopus.com/inward/record.url?eid=2-

s2.0002295751 0partnerID=40md5=afl0f41984977b2fb5394f41a5c42a67

[21] M. Luessi, M. Eichmann, G. M. Schuster, and A. K. Katsaggelos, "Framework for efficient optimal multilevel image thresholding," Journal of Electronic Imaging, vol. 18, no. 1, 2009, pp. 013 004–013 004–10. [Online]. Available: http://dx.doi.org/10.1117/1.3073891

[22] N. Otsu, "A Threshold Selection Method from Gray-Level Histograms," IEEE Transactions on Systems, Man and Cybernetics, vol. 9, no. 1, January 1979, pp. 62–66.

[23] M. Sezgin and B. Sankur, "Survey over image thresholding techniques and quantitative performance evaluation." Journal of Electronic Imaging, 2004, pp. 146–165.

[24] L. Chen, ". laplacian embedded regression for scalable manifold regularization," Neural Networks and Learning Systems, IEEE Transactions, vol. 23, 2012, pp. 902–915.

[25] G. Shrivakshan and C. Chandrasekar, "A comparison of various edge detection techniques used in image processing," IJCSI International Journal of Computer Science Issues, vol. 9, no. 1, September 2012, pp. 269–276.

Remote Sensing of Temperature-Stress Coupled Effects

Simone Boccardi, Giovanni Maria Carlomagno, Carosena Meola
Department of Industrial Engineering - Aerospace Division, University of Naples Federico II, Naples, Italy
e-mail: simone.boccardi@unina.it, carmagno@unina.it, carmeola@unina.it

***Abstract*— The aim of this paper is concerned with the use of an infrared imaging device to measure the very small temperature variations which are linked to thermo-elastic effects. The latter are associated with material volume variations undergone by a cantilever beam under cyclic bending load. This is a difficult task since the temperature variations are very small and at the edge of the instrument resolution. However, with the aid of a reference sample it is possible to eliminate most of the instrumental and environmental noise so as to obtain reliable measurements. This method allows extending the use of an infrared imaging device outside its resolution range.**

Keywords-infrared thermography; cyclic bending; thermo-elastic effect; temperature variation; radiation sensing.

I. Introduction

Temperature represents a key parameter in almost all the industrial processes. In particular, owing to composite materials, the production of a sound laminate strongly depends on the processing temperature. In fact, the polymerization cycle of a thermoset matrix based composite is generally performed in autoclave and strongly depends on the temperature ramp and absolute value. However, temperature is important also for the forming of a laminate involving a thermoplastic matrix. The possibility to obtain a laminate free, or of low content, of porosity strongly depends on the combination of temperature and pressure during the fabrication process. In these cases the temperature values to be controlled are quite high and measurable with different types of sensors.

It is not easy to measure very small temperature variations, which can be easily affected by the several sources of error that are always present and which become progressively more important as the quantity to be measured becomes smaller. Of course, the measure becomes more complex in the presence of dynamic, or unsteady, phenomena. As an example, trying to measure the temperature variations, which develop over the surface of a cantilever beam under cyclic bending tests, may be a very difficult task.

This measure appears complex from two points of view. On one side, depending on the material under test, the temperature amplitude may be very small. On the other side, the temperature variations are generated by the oscillation of the sample and depend on its geometry.

Then, no contact sensors are allowed since their presence can alter the geometry and jeopardize the measurement. In addition, contact sensors suffer from contact resistance and are vulnerable to thermal conduction effects, which also affect the measurement accuracy. The only solution may be to perform measurements through remote detection of thermal radiation, which mainly means with infrared thermography (IRT). Indeed, IRT thanks to its non-contact character and its multifarious applications, is consolidating increasing attention from both the industrial and academic communities.

In particular, IRT has proved its capability to visualize the surface temperature variations, associated with thermo-elastic/plastic effects, which are experienced by a body under load [1][2]. These temperature variations supply information useful for assessing the material's characteristics and performance. This represents a great advantage since it makes possible getting information on the material by simply monitoring it under load. This can be done using the thermo-elastic equation [3], which expresses the change in temperature (ΔT) of a solid in terms of the change of the sum of the principal stresses ($\Delta\sigma$). In particular, under adiabatic conditions, positive dilatation (tension) entails cooling of the material and vice-versa.

In this regard, a difficult task is to perceive the temperature variations which develop under relatively low loads. In these circumstances, a detector able to sense the small difference in thermal radiation, associated with light surface temperature variations, is required. Previous works [4][5] showed that a long wave (LW) quantum well infrared photodetector (QWIP) is well suited for sensing the small thermal radiation associated with thermo-elastic phenomena, but the QWIP is affected by noise, mainly dark current, effects [5]. This noise exhibits a random temporal character that cannot be easily removed through the commonly in use signal restoration methods. Conversely, it seems that it can be accounted for and suppressed in a simple manner with the use of a reference area [4][5].

The aim of this work is to further investigate the reference-area method by highlighting its potential and likely limitations for a better exploitation of infrared imaging devices in presence of feeble thermal radiation.

Apart from the introduction, the structure of this paper includes four sections. In particular, a description of the test setup and the testing procedure is given in Section II, to follow in Section III with some theoretical hints, which justify the use of infrared thermography to monitor cyclic bending tests. Section IV, which represents the core of the work, is involved with post-processing of thermographic images. In particular, it is shown how the reference area method is effective to account for and eliminate most of the instrument and environmental noise; this is illustrated with some key examples. The work ends with some concluding remarks and future trends.

II. EXPERIMENTAL

The reference-area method can be deployed in different applications and for different purposes. In the following, an example of application concerning cyclic bending tests is illustrated. This involves the measurement of very small temperature variations and is well suited for the purpose.

A. Test Setup and Procedure

The test setup is shown in Fig. 1. The specimen bending is operated with an electro mechanical actuator through a taut wire and a return spring. As it can be seen, two specimens are clamped nearby on their bottom side (fixture) as cantilever beams. One remains unloaded and is used as source to apply the reference-area method. The other one (the specimen under test) is inserted, with its upper end, into a clip attached to the wire which forces the specimen to bend back and forth under the wire alternate displacement.

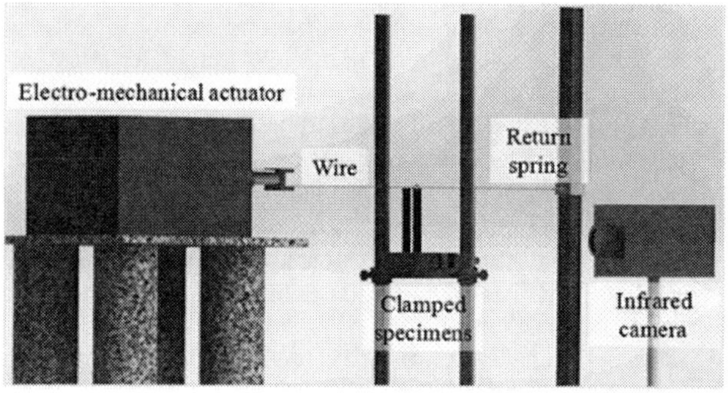

Figure 1. Setup for cyclic bending tests

The infrared camera is positioned so as to see both specimens at once (from one surface). The used infrared camera is the SC6000 (Flir systems), which is equipped with a QWIP detector, working in the 8-9 μm infrared band, NEDT < 35 mK, spatial resolution 640x512 pixels full frame with the pixel size 25 μm x 25 μm and with a windowing option linked to frequency frame rate and temperature range. Sequences of thermal images are acquired during loading, or better, to allow for a complete visualization of thermal effects evolution with respect to the ambient temperature, the acquisition starts few seconds before load application and lasts for some time after.

III. SOME THEORETICAL REMARKS

The case study involves variations of temperature induced by thermo-elastic effects, which can be traced to the classical thermo-elastic equation, formulated by Biot [3]:

$$\Delta T = -KT_a \, \Delta\sigma \tag{1}$$

which expresses the change of temperature (ΔT) of a solid in terms of the change of the sum of the principal stresses ($\Delta\sigma$). In particular, T_a is the absolute body temperature, $\Delta\sigma$ is the mean stress amplitude, and K is the material thermo-elastic constant. Equation (1) relates the temperature variations to the volume variations and applies to isotropic materials under reversible and adiabatic conditions (i.e., in the elastic regime and neglecting heat transfer within the body and to the environment). Under adiabatic conditions, positive dilatation (tension) entails cooling of the material and vice-versa.

The interest is to extract ΔT values from the sequences recorded during cyclic bending. The amplitude of ΔT values, for a given material, depends mainly on the location over the specimen length, i.e., the distance from the fixture and on the bending frequency if temperature relaxation occurs.

IV. IMAGE PROCESSING AND DATA ANALYSIS

The recorded sequences undergo post-processing by using the Flir ResearchIR software (available from the Flir systems package) and specific routines developed in the Matlab environment [4]. The first image (t = 0 s) of the sequence, i.e. the specimen surface at ambient temperature, before starting of loading, is subtracted to each subsequent image so as to generate a map of temperature difference ΔT:

$$\Delta T(i,j,t) = T(i,j,t) - T(i,j,0) \tag{2}$$

i and j representing lines and columns of the surface temperature array. Several measurement positions, as depicted in Fig. 2, are considered over solicited (A) and unsolicited (P1, P2, P3) specimens.

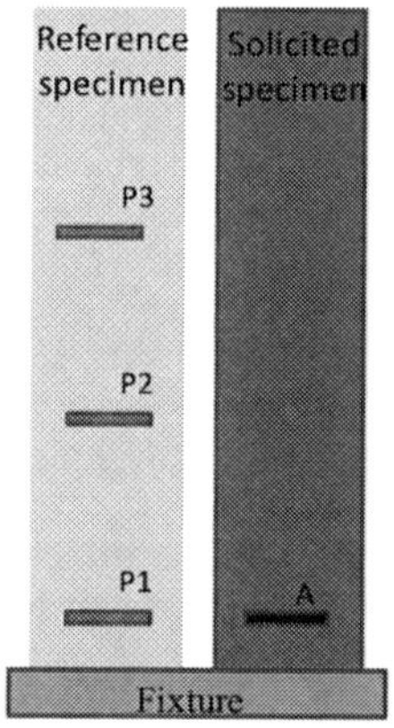

Figure 2. Sketch of measurement positions over the two specimens

A. Some Examples

A ΔT plot is extracted in the position A (i.e., close to the fixture) and is shown in Fig. 3. In more details, the resulting curve corresponds to the mean value in an area of width 40 pixels and height 20 pixels by suppressing, of course, border appraisals. This plot refers to the original raw signal ΔT_R taken with cyclic bending at a frequency f_b = 0.8 Hz. As it can be seen, ΔT_R displays quasi-sinusoidal variations coupled with the cyclic load; more specifically ΔT_R goes up and down following the alternate tension/compression load. However, the sinusoidal trend is not a regular one, but disrupted by a jumping-like effect that is due to the instrument noise [5].

To separately account for the instrument noise ΔT_N, a plot is meanwhile extracted on the unloaded reference specimen and shown in Fig. 4. In particular, the ΔT_N curve corresponds to the mean value in the P1 zone, which is placed at the same distance from the fixture of the zone A and has its same dimensions (see Fig. 2).

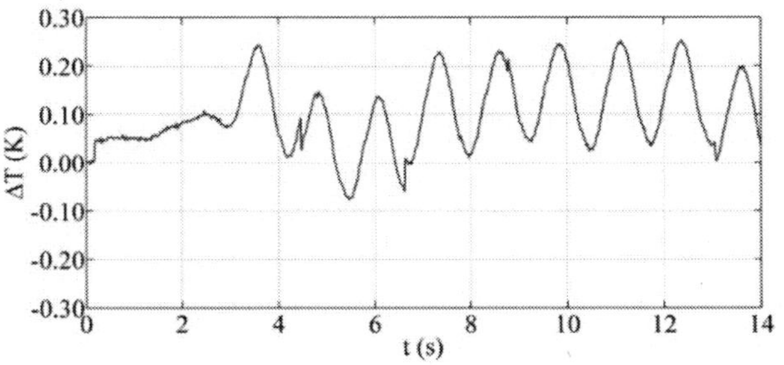

Figure 3. ΔT_R plot for f_b = 0.8 Hz

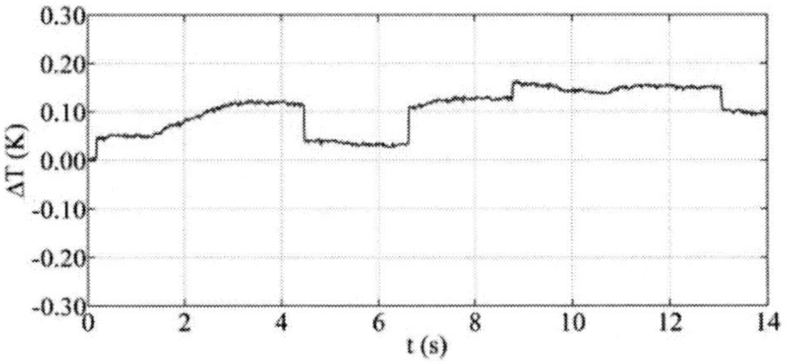

Figure 4. ΔT_N plot over the unloaded specimen

By comparing Fig. 4 to Fig. 3, it is possible to clearly distinguish the detrimental effects the random noise has on the quasi-sinusoidal pattern. Such effects include macro (jumps) and micro (slight slopes) scale phenomena. The two plots ΔT_R and ΔT_N are characterized by the same trend, even if they are extracted from two different zones, i.e. one on the specimen under test (Fig. 3) and the other one on the reference specimen (Fig. 4).

As a major effect, the quasi-sinusoid has lost the alignment of peaks and valleys with respect to the horizontal axis. These displacements of the ΔT_R signal are perfectly coupled with the position of ramps and jumps in the ΔT_N signal. In particular, by looking at the first portion of Fig. 3 within the first 2.5 seconds (before starting of the bending) it is possible to see that, by changing zone, the noise amplitude remains the same. In fact, on both graphs, $\Delta T = 0$ for t = 0, but soon after ΔT undergoes an abrupt rise, followed by a steadiness and then a ramp.

To better underline this aspect, three ΔT_N plots, taken in three different zones P1, P2 and P3, are compared in Fig. 5. As depicted in Fig. 2, the three zones are differently displaced along the reference specimen, with care to avoid boundary effects. In particular, P1 represents the zone from where the ΔT_N signal already shown in Fig. 3 has been extracted.

Looking at Fig. 5 it is possible to see that the three signals are practically superimposed. More specifically, they are perfectly superimposed with regards to the appearance of jumps in time, which means the macro-scale temporal noise. Instead, small variations of amplitude can be discriminated by changing zone. Such variations may be ascribed to several factors involving either the spatial noise of the instrument, or environmental noise, or surface emissivity changes. This type of noise, whatever its origin, is very small and surely negligible with respect to the major temporal component.

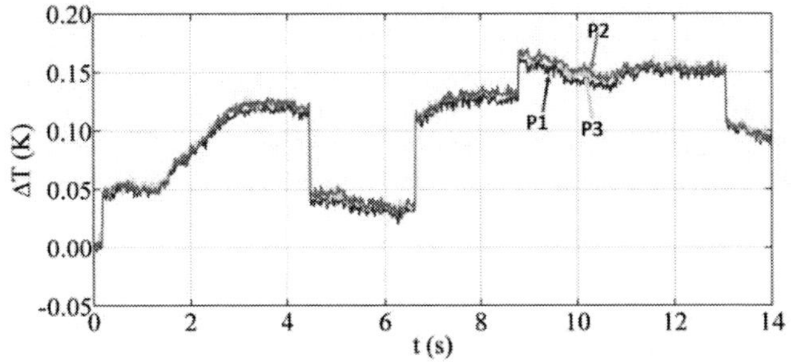

Figure 5. ΔT_N plot in three places over the unloaded specimen

B. *Noise Correction*

First of all, the correction is intended to eliminate temporal noise while spatial noise is considered as negligible. The noise can be eliminated through correction by the use of the unloaded reference specimen [4]. The signal in the reference specimen, which accounts for the noise ΔT_N, is subtracted from the original raw signal ΔT_R. Then, the corrected ΔT_C signal is obtained as:

$$\Delta T_C = \Delta T_R - \Delta T_N \quad (3)$$

An example of corrected ΔT_C signal is shown in Fig. 6, which is practically the result of the subtraction of Fig. 4 from Fig. 3. As it can be seen, the noise is eliminated and a sinusoidal pattern is practically recovered, which perfectly synchronizes with the specimen alternate displacement. In addition, also the constant (on the average) $\Delta T = 0$ value in the first portion before starting of the load is recovered.

It is worth underlining that the correction method appears able to eliminate different types of noise: the jumps effect, but also the slight ramp effect like that present in the first portion of the ΔT_R signal of Fig. 3.

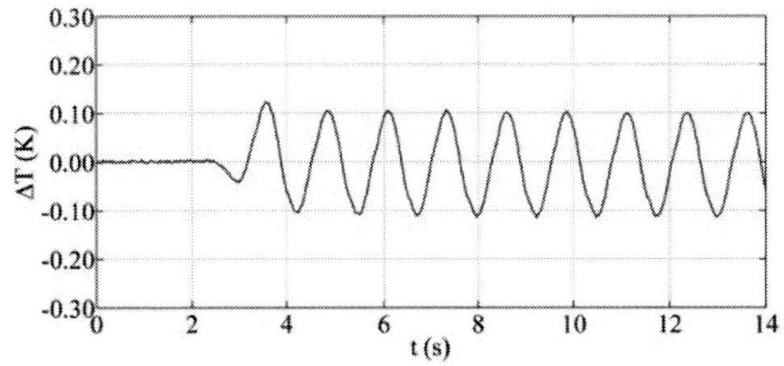

Figure 6. Corrected ΔT_C plot for f_b = 0.8 Hz

Of course, the noise effects become ever more pronounced as the ΔT amplitude decreases. Thus, to further investigate the effectiveness of the reference-area method, a much lower amplitude signal is analyzed. This signal is obtained by recording thermal images in time sequence during cyclic bending at the lower frequency of $f_b = 0.05$ Hz. The three signals ΔT_R, ΔT_N, and ΔT_C are compared in Fig. 7.

The first thing to notice is the predominant effect of the instrument noise. In fact, by comparing Fig. 7a to Fig. 7b, it is practically impossible to distinguish any difference between ΔT_R and ΔT_N trends, or better between the solicited specimen and the unsolicited one. It is worth noting that the ΔT_R signal has been recorded with a specimen undergoing cyclic bending at frequency $f_b = 0.05$ Hz and deflection $D_F = \pm 7.5$ mm. The temperature variations associated within this pair of parameters are very small and then, it is normal to see the noise fluctuations to prevailing and completely disrupting the sinusoidal pattern (Fig. 7a) produced by the thermo-elastic effects. Surprisingly, the sinusoidal pattern is again recovered (Fig. 7c), through correction with the reference-area method.

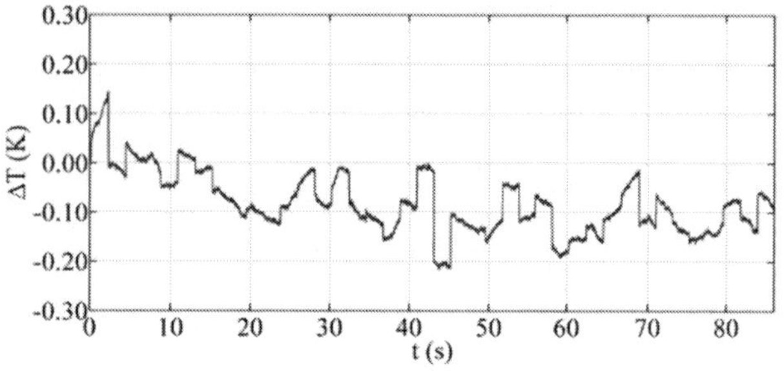

a) ΔT_R

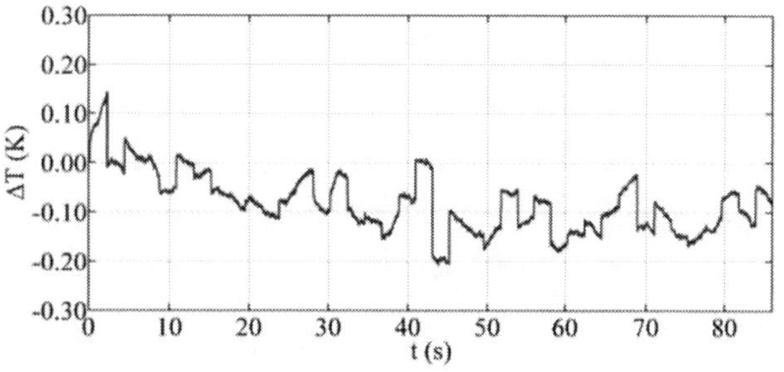

b) ΔT_N

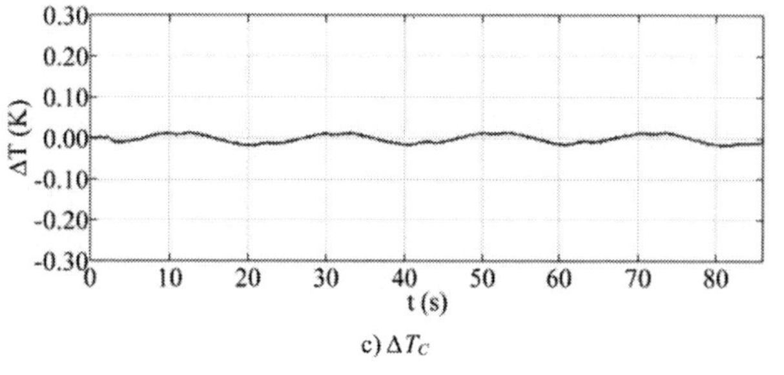

c) ΔT_C

Figure 7. ΔT_R , ΔT_N and ΔT_C plot for bending at $f_b = 0.05$ Hz

However, the resulting ΔT_C signal is very small to be exploited for material characterization purposes. In fact, it is affected by heat transfer mechanisms and other phenomena, which should be taken into account to make the ΔT values usable, but this is outside the aim of this work and is not herein discussed.

V. Conclusion and Future Work

Through some practical examples, it has been shown that it is possible to use an infrared imaging device to detect and also evaluate also the feeble thermal radiation, which is of the same order of magnitude as the instrument noise and that is commonly considered outside the instrument resolution range. In particular, it has been demonstrated that this is possible with the help of a reference area, which allows for estimation of the instrument noise. Then, the noise is separately evaluated and eliminated from the raw signal.

It is worth noting that cyclic bending tests have herein been used as reference, for convenience, since the sinusoidal pattern coupled with the specimen alternate displacement is well suited to demonstrate the validity of the method. In fact, by changing the bending frequency and so the amplitude of the sinusoid, it has been possible to visualize noise effects of different types and of different orders of magnitude. In addition, the capability of the method to either restore a fairly affected curve, or recover a completely destroyed one, has been demonstrated.

Conversely, this method can be exploited in a broader context whenever the measurement of small variations of temperature is required. Of course, this method may be applied to a larger extent, even in the presence of not-too-small values that are less affected by noise. It is worth nothing that the possibility to perform measurements with a remote imaging device offers countless benefits. Amongst them, it prevents any alterations to the testing objet and to the quantity to be measured. But, it eliminates also the trouble of placing a great number of contact sensors and managing with cables. As a last point, it can be inferred that, with the application of this simple method, it becomes possible to resolve small variations of temperature, which may be otherwise impossible.

As future work, we will investigate other study cases such as monitoring composite materials under impact tests with an infrared imaging device. Indeed, due to the ever broad deployment and development of composites, assessing their resistance under impact is of great concern to both academic and industrial communities. While it has already been demonstrated the capability of infrared thermography to catch thermal signatures induced by impact tests [6][7], outlining in an accurate way the boundaries between sound and damaged zones remains still an open question. This task, due to the small size of temperature variations at these boundaries, may benefit of the application of the reference area method. On the other hand, the evaluation of the extension of the damaged zone is very useful for material design purposes to assess the material performance.

However, in the future, this method may be improved and exploited in other study cases to get the best from thermographic images also in consideration of the vast variety of applications which may be addressed with infrared thermography.

REFERENCES

[1] C. Meola, G.M. Carlomagno. "Infrared thermography to impact-driven thermal effects" Applied Physics A, vol. 96, pp. 759-762, 2009.

[2] C. Meola, G.M. Carlomagno, C. Bonavolontà, M. Valentino, "Monitoring composites under bending tests with infrared thermography" Advances in Optical Technologies, vol. 2012, (7 pages) 2012.

[3] M.A. Biot, "Thermoelasticity and irreversible thermodynamics" Journal of Applied Physics, vol. 27, pp. 240- 253, 1956.

[4] S. Boccardi, G.M. Carlomagno, C. Bonavolontà, M. Valentino, C. Meola, "Infrared thermography to monitor Glare® under cyclic bending tests with correction of camera noise" Proc. QIRT 2014, Bordeaux, France, 7-11 July 2014.

[5] C. Meola, S. Boccardi, G.M. Carlomagno, "Measurements of very small temperature variations with LWIR QWIP infrared camera", Infrared Physics and Technology, vol. 72, pp. 195-203, 2015.

[6] C. Meola, G.M. Carlomagno, "Impact damage in GFRP: new insights with Infrared Thermography", Composites Part A, vol.41, pp. 1839-1847, 2010.

[7] S. Boccardi, G.M. Carlomagno, C. Meola, P. Russo, G. Simeoli, "Monitoring impact damaging of thermoplastic composites", Journal of Physics: Conference Series 658 (2015) (XXII AIVELA Annual Meeting) 012005 doi:10.1088/1742-6596/658/1/012005.

AUTHOR INDEX